WORD MAX 1 5300

WorldCom Edu

WORD MAX 5300 1

초판	2016년 10월 31일
지은이	김 지 훈, 김 채 원
영문검수	Kenneth Drenen
책임편집	신 은 진
편집팀	월드컴 에듀 편집팀
펴낸이	임 병 업
디자인	임 예 슬, 김 지 현, 차 지 원
펴낸곳	(주)월드컴 에듀
등록	2016년 10월 31일
주소	서울시 강남구 남부순환로 2706, 5층 (도곡동, 차우빌딩)
전화	02)3273-4300(대표)
팩스	02)3273-4303
홈페이지	www.wcbooks.co.kr
이메일	wc4300@wcbooks.co.kr

WORD MAX 5300 여는 글

언어를 배울 때 어휘 학습은 모든 언어 학습자가 가장 먼저 시작하는 분야이면서 동시에 가장 숙달하기 어려운 분야입니다. 이는 문법이나 읽기, 듣기와는 다른 어휘 학습의 독특한 측면이며 다른 학습 방식이 필요한 이유이기도 합니다. 수능을 비롯한 최근의 영어 시험 경향은 결국 어휘사용능력이 전반적인 문제 해결의 핵심 요소가 되고 있습니다.
WORD MAX 5300은 최신 경향에 맞추어 가장 효율적인 어휘 학습 방식을 제공하고자 합니다.

WORD MAX 5300시리즈는
과학적인 방법으로 최대의 효과를 얻을 수 있도록 어휘를 엄선했습니다.

WORD MAX 5300시리즈는 총 6권의 수준별 구성으로 최신 출제 경향과 엄선된 예문 및 다양하고 풍부한 리뷰 테스트를 통해 어휘 활용 능력을 최대화 할 수 있도록 구성했습니다.
최근 12년의 수능 및 각종 시험 기출 문제와 교과서 자료를 중심으로 자체 데이터베이스를 통해 학습 대상 어휘를 엄선했습니다. 특히 기출 빈도와 출제 예상도를 고려하여 선정한 어휘들은 효율적인 어휘 학습을 도와 줄 것입니다.

단계별로 세분화되고 실용성 있는 어휘 학습 환경을 제공합니다.

Level 1~3은 핵심적인 어휘를 풍부한 예문과 리뷰 테스트를 통해 예비중학 과정부터 중등 내신 대비까지 학생들의 기본적 영어 능력 향상에 도움이 되도록 구성했습니다.
Level 4~6은 최근 12년간의 수학능력시험, 모의고사, 학력평가의 기출문제를 토대로 어휘를 선정하였습니다. 더불어 각 어휘의 출제 맥락을 연구하고 수준별 분류 및 보정과정을 통해 단순 어휘 학습을 넘어 전반적인 영어 활용 능력을 향상 시킬 수 있게 구성했습니다.

다양한 어휘 활용 연습 기회를 제공하여 전반적인 영어 실력의 향상을 목표로 합니다.

WORD MAX 5300시리즈는 일일 테스트를 비롯한 Review Test의 총 8개 섹션의 다양한 테스트를 통해 학습한 어휘를 완전히 이해하고 활용할 수 있도록 했습니다. 쓰임에 따라 다양한 뜻을 가진 어휘들과 이에 대한 실용성 높은 예문들은 영어 사용 능력 향상에 확실한 도움이 될 것입니다.

어휘 학습 방법에 대한 이견은 많지만 어휘 학습 대상 선정의 중요성에 대해서는 연구자와 일선 교육자 모두 공감하고 있습니다. WORD MAX 5300시리즈를 충실히 학습한다면 어휘를 학습하는 재미 뿐만 아니라 영어 전반에서 실력 향상을 성취 할 수 있을 것이라 자부합니다.

WORD MAX 5300시리즈와 함께 어휘 학습에 최고의 결과를 얻을 수 있기를 기원합니다.

- 월드컴 에듀 편집팀 일동

구성 및 활용

1 단계별 30일 구성의 계획적 어휘 학습!

'단어 → 어구 → 예문' 순으로 자연스럽게 확장되는 학습을 통해 어휘력을 향상합니다.

하루 20개
단계별 30일 구성

동사의 3단 변화형과 비교형 제시를 통해
시제별 동사 형태를 연습합니다.

다양한 예문을 통해
표제어를 응용 학습합니다.

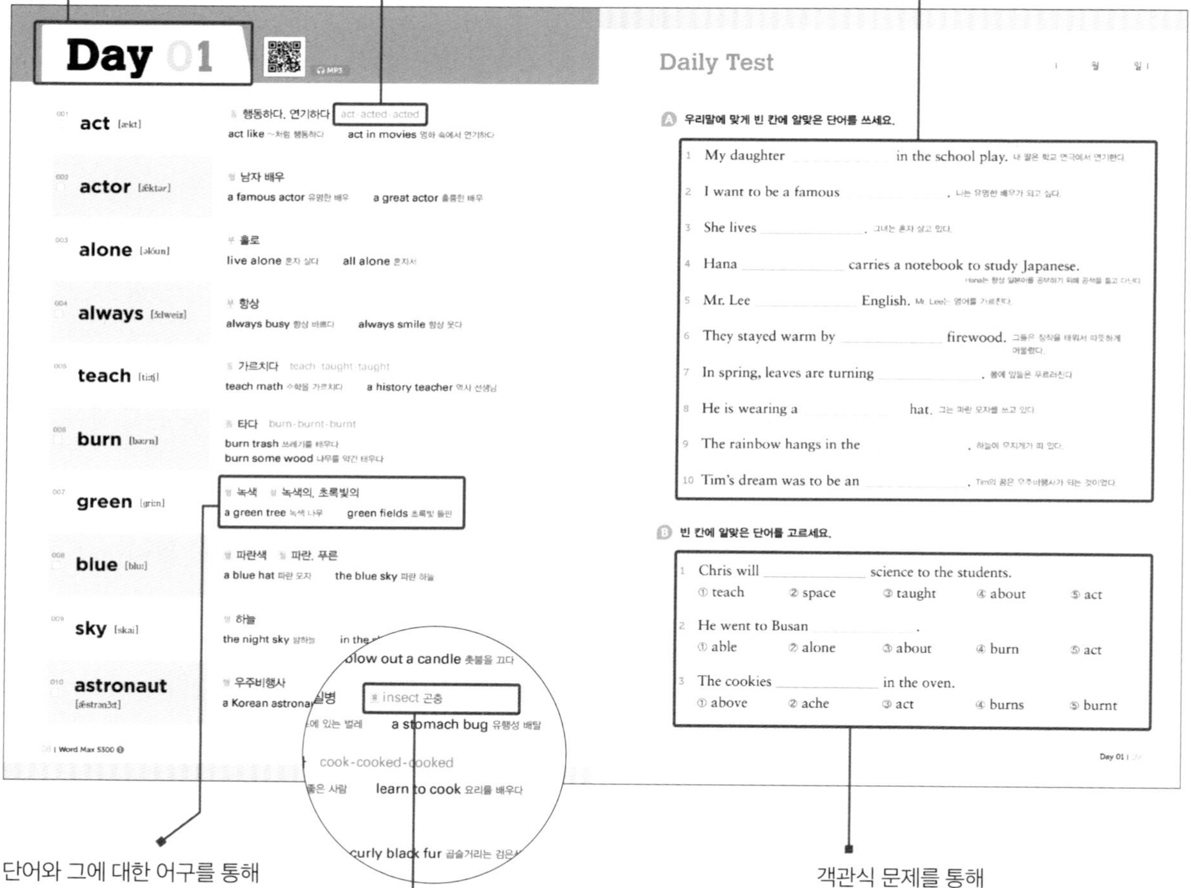

단어와 그에 대한 어구를 통해
다양한 어휘 학습을 가능하게 합니다.

유의어, 반의어, 연관 단어 등의
제시를 통해 어휘력을 확장합니다.

객관식 문제를 통해
내신대비 어휘학습을 가능하게 합니다.

2 Review Test 7가지 유형으로 학습 점검하기!

2일마다 학습한 어휘를 다양한 유형의 문제를 통해 반복 학습합니다.

어구 빈칸 완성
우리말에 따라 어구를 완성합니다

영영 풀이
보기에서 영영 풀이에 해당하는 단어를 찾아봅니다.

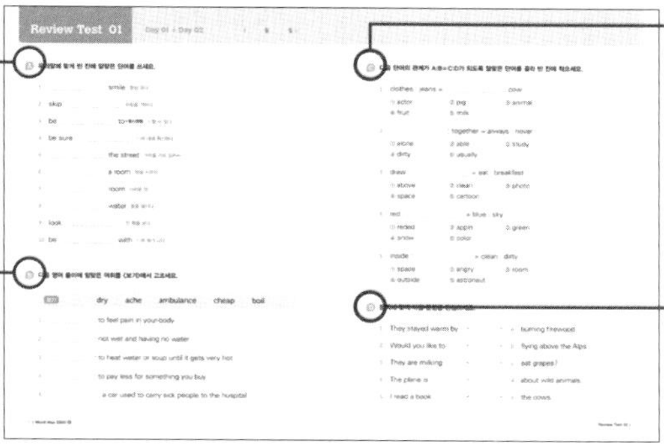

어휘 관계 파악
단어 간의 관계를 파악하여 알맞은 단어를 찾아봅니다.

문장 연결 완성
문맥상 알맞은 문장끼리 연결하여 완성된 문장을 학습합니다.

영영 어휘활용
문장에서 문맥상 알맞은 단어를 선택합니다.

문장 완성
우리말에 따라 보기에서 알맞은 단어를 골라 문장을 완성합니다.

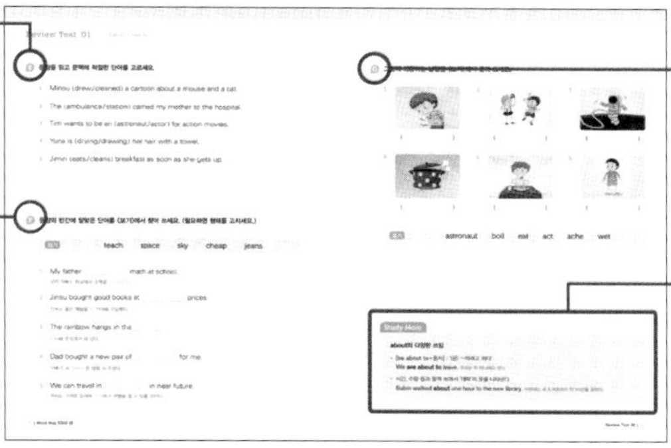

그림-단어 연결
각 그림에 알맞은 단어를 찾아봅니다.

Study More
표제어에 대한 확장된 개념을 제시함으로써 다양한 관점에서 어휘력을 향상 시킬 수 있습니다.

3 Work Book

워크북을 활용하여 단어의 철자와 뜻을 한번 더 반복 학습합니다.

쓰기 노트

일일 테스트

목차

★ 책 속의 책 Workbook 제공

WORD MAX 1 5300

Day 01

MP3

001 □ **act** [ækt]

동 행동하다, 연기하다 act-acted-acted

act like ~처럼 행동하다 act in movies 영화 속에서 연기하다

002 □ **actor** [ǽktər]

명 남자 배우

a famous actor 유명한 배우 a great actor 훌륭한 배우

003 □ **alone** [əlóun]

부 홀로

live alone 혼자 살다 all alone 혼자서

004 □ **always** [ɔ́ːlweiz]

부 항상

always busy 항상 바쁘다 always smile 항상 웃다

005 □ **teach** [tiːtʃ]

동 가르치다 teach-taught-taught

teach math 수학을 가르치다 a history teacher 역사 선생님

006 □ **burn** [bəːrn]

동 타다 burn-burnt-burnt

burn trash 쓰레기를 태우다
burn some wood 나무를 약간 태우다

007 □ **green** [griːn]

명 녹색 형 녹색의, 초록빛의

a green tree 녹색 나무 green fields 초록빛 들판

008 □ **blue** [bluː]

명 파란색 형 파란, 푸른

a blue hat 파란 모자 the blue sky 파란 하늘

009 □ **sky** [skai]

명 하늘

the night sky 밤하늘 in the sky 하늘에서

010 □ **astronaut** [ǽstrənɔ̀ːt]

명 우주비행사 유 spaceman 우주비행사

a Korean astronaut 한국인 우주비행사

Daily Test

| 월 일 |

A 우리말에 맞게 빈 칸에 알맞은 단어를 쓰세요.

1 My daughter ____________ in the school play. 내 딸은 학교 연극에서 연기한다.

2 I want to be a famous ____________. 나는 유명한 배우가 되고 싶다.

3 She lives ____________. 그녀는 혼자 살고 있다.

4 Hana ____________ carries a notebook to study Japanese. Hana는 항상 일본어를 공부하기 위해 공책을 들고 다닌다.

5 Mr. Lee ____________ English. Mr. Lee는 영어를 가르친다.

6 They stayed warm by ____________ firewood. 그들은 장작을 태워서 따뜻하게 머물렀다.

7 In spring, leaves are turning ____________. 봄에 잎들은 푸르러진다.

8 He is wearing a ____________ hat. 그는 파란 모자를 쓰고 있다.

9 The rainbow hangs in the ____________. 하늘에 무지개가 떠 있다.

10 Tim's dream was to be an ____________. Tim의 꿈은 우주비행사가 되는 것이었다.

B 빈 칸에 알맞은 단어를 고르세요.

1 Chris will ____________ science to the students.

① teach ② space ③ taught ④ about ⑤ act

2 He went to Busan ____________.

① able ② alone ③ about ④ burn ⑤ act

3 The cookies ____________ in the oven.

① above ② ache ③ act ④ burns ⑤ burnt

Day 01

MP3

011 **space** [speis]

명 우주

a space station 우주 정거장　　in space 우주에서

012 **album** [ǽlbəm]

명 앨범

a photo album 사진첩　　a wedding album 웨딩 앨범

013 **grape** [greip]

명 포도

grape juice 포도 주스　　grow grapes 포도를 재배하다

014 **apple** [ǽpl]

명 사과

an apple tree 사과 나무　　Big Apple 뉴욕

015 **able** [éibl]

형 ~할 수 있는

be able to+동사원형 ~할 수 있다
be able to speak English 영어를 말 할 수 있다

016 **about** [əbáut]

전 ~에 관해서

be sure about ~에 대해 확신하다
a book about flowers 꽃에 대한 책

017 **above** [əbʌ́v]

전 ~의 위에

above the clouds 구름 위에　　above the hill 언덕 위에

018 **ache** [eik]

명 아픔　동 아프다, 쑤시다

have a headache 두통이 있다
His left leg ached. 그의 왼쪽 다리가 아팠다.

019 **across** [əkrɔ́:s]

전 ~을 가로질러

across from ~의 맞은편에　　across the street 거리를 가로 질러서

020 **ambulance** [ǽmbjələns]

명 구급차

call an ambulance 구급차를 부르다
the ambulance service 구급차 서비스

Daily Test

| 월 일 |

A 우리말에 맞게 빈 칸에 알맞은 단어를 쓰세요.

1 NASA is planning to build a ______________ station.
NASA는 우주 정거장을 세울 예정이다.

2 Tom made a photo ______________ for his mother.
Tom은 그의 엄마를 위해서 사진첩을 만들었다.

3 Would you like to eat some ______________? 포도를 좀 드시겠어요?

4 The ______ - ______ is my favorite fruit. 사과는 내가 가장 좋아하는 과일이다.

5 He is ______________ to understand the question. 그는 그 문제를 이해 할 수 있다.

6 We're not sure ______________ this part. 우리는 이 부분에 대해 확신할 수 없다.

7 The plane is flying ______________ the Alps. 비행기는 알프스 산 위를 날고 있다.

8 I have a ______________. 나는 배가 아프다.

9 Jim and his dog are walking ______________ the street.
Jim과 그의 강아지는 거리를 가로질러 걷고 있다.

10 My father called an ______________ for my grandfather.
아버지는 할아버지를 위해 구급차를 불렀다.

B 빈 칸에 알맞은 단어를 고르세요.

1 I am ______________ to swim.
① can ② space ③ able ④ across ⑤ burn

2 The bird is flying ______________ the bridge.
① above ② able ③ sky ④ taught ⑤ in

3 He ran ______________ the garden to catch the cat.
① up ② above ③ forward ④ out ⑤ across

Day 02

MP3

021 ☐ **clothes** [klouðz]
명 옷
casual clothes 평상복　　baby clothes 아기용 옷

022 ☐ **jeans** [dʒiːnz]
명 청바지
blue jeans 청바지　　wear jeans 청바지를 입다

023 ☐ **animal** [ǽnəməl]
명 동물
wild animals 야생 동물　　the animal kingdom 동물의 왕국

024 ☐ **cow** [kau]
명 소
cows on the farm 농장에 있는 소　　cow's milk 소의 우유

025 ☐ **clean** [kliːn]
형 깨끗한　동 청소하다　clean-cleaned-cleaned
clean air 깨끗한 공기　　clean a room 방을 치우다

026 ☐ **dirty** [də́ːrti]
형 더러운
a dirty room 더러운 방　　dirty clothes 더러운 옷

027 ☐ **cheap** [tʃiːp]
형 값이 싼
a cheap shirt 값이 싼 셔츠　　a cheap restaurant 값이 싼 식당

028 ☐ **expensive** [ikspénsiv]
형 비싼
an expensive car 비싼 자동차
an expensive jacket 비싼 자켓

029 ☐ **dry** [drai]
형 마른, 건조한　동 말리다
dry weather 건조한 날씨
Dry your hands first! 손을 먼저 말려라!

030 ☐ **wet** [wet]
형 젖은
wet clothes 젖은 옷　　get wet 물에 젖다

Daily Test

| 월 일 |

A 우리말에 맞게 빈 칸에 알맞은 단어를 쓰세요.

1 I bought some new ______________ yesterday. 나는 어제 새 옷 몇 벌을 샀다.

2 Sally wears blue ______________ today. Sally는 오늘 청바지를 입고 있다.

3 There are a variety of ______________ in the zoo. 동물원에 다양한 동물들이 있다.

4 They are milking the ______________. 그들은 소의 젖을 짜고 있다.

5 I should ______________ up the living room. 나는 거실을 치워야 한다.

6 Wash your ______________ hands. 더러워진 손을 씻으세요.

7 This coat is ______________. 그 코트는 가격이 싸다.

8 The chair was too ______________. 그 의자는 너무 비쌌다.

9 Yuna is ______________ her hair. 유나는 그녀의 머리를 말리는 중이다.

10 The cat got ______________ in the rain. 고양이는 빗물에 젖었다.

B 빈 칸에 알맞은 단어를 고르세요.

1 The diamond necklace is very ______________.

① alone ② expensive ③ angry ④ inside ⑤ eat

2 We'll help you ______________ the house.

① clean ② ache ③ cheap ④ boil ⑤ cow

3 The car is very ______________.

① dry ② draw ③ clothes ④ happy ⑤ cheap

Day 02

MP3

031 **character** [kǽriktər]
명 인물, 성격
a cartoon character 만화 등장인물　a main character 주요 인물

032 **draw** [drɔː]
동 그리다　draw-drew-drawn
draw a picture 그림을 그리다　draw a cartoon 만화를 그리다

033 **breakfast** [brékfəst]
명 아침 식사
eat breakfast 아침을 먹다　skip breakfast 아침 식사를 거르다

034 **eat** [iːt]
동 먹다　eat-ate-eaten
eat too much 너무 많이 먹다　something to eat 먹을 것

035 **boil** [bɔil]
동 끓이다　boil-boiled-boiled
boil water 물을 끓이다　boil soup 수프를 끓이다

036 **borrow** [bάrou]
동 빌리다　borrow-borrowed-borrowed
borrow a pen 펜을 빌리다
borrow Tim's umbrella Tim의 우산을 빌리다

037 **book** [buk]
명 책
read a book 책을 읽다
a book about wild animals 야생동물에 관한 책

038 **inside** [insáid]
명 내부　전 안쪽에
the inside of the classroom 교실 내부　look inside 안 쪽을 보다

039 **outside** [àutsáid]
명 겉, 바깥쪽　형 외부의
the outside walls 바깥쪽 벽
the outside of the building 빌딩 외부

040 **angry** [ǽŋgri]
형 화가 난
get angry 화나다　be angry with ~에 화가 나다

Daily Test

| 월 일 |

A 우리말에 맞게 빈 칸에 알맞은 단어를 쓰세요.

1 The little prince is the main ______________ of the story. 어린 왕자는 이 이야기의 주요 인물이다.

2 Minsu ______________ a cartoon. 민수는 만화를 그렸다.

3 I eat ______________ at 7:30. 나는 7시 30분에 아침을 먹는다.

4 Jinsu does not like to ______________ vegetables. 진수는 야채를 먹는 것을 싫어한다.

5 Grandmother ______________ soup for me. 할머니는 나를 위해 수프를 끓여주셨다.

6 Can I ______________ your notebook? 너의 공책을 좀 빌릴 수 있을까?

7 I read a ______________ about wild animals. 나는 야생동물에 관한 책을 읽었다.

8 There are cookies ______________ the box. 상자 안에 쿠키들이 있다.

9 I walked around the ______________ of the castle. 나는 성 밖 주변을 걸었다.

10 Ted got really ______________ with his sister. Ted는 그의 여동생 때문에 화가 났다.

B 빈 칸에 알맞은 단어를 고르세요.

1 She ______________ some water in a pot.
① boiled ② wet ③ borrow ④ inside ⑤ drew

2 Can I ______________ your umbrella?
① cheap ② outside ③ angry ④ dirty ⑤ borrow

3 It's raining! Let's go ______________!
① inside ② dirty ③ clothes ④ jeans ⑤ boil

Review Test 01

Day 01 + Day 02 | 월 일 |

A 우리말에 맞게 빈 칸에 알맞은 단어를 쓰세요.

1 ________________ smile 항상 웃다

2 skip ________________ 아침을 거르다

3 be ________________ to+동사원형 ~할 수 있다

4 be sure ________________ ~에 대해 확신하다

5 ________________ the street 거리를 가로 질러서

6 ________________ a room 방을 치우다

7 ________________ room 더러운 방

8 ________________ water 물을 끓이다

9 look ________________ 안 쪽을 보다

10 be ________________ with ~에 화가 나다

B 다음 영어 풀이에 알맞은 어휘를 〈보기〉에서 고르세요.

보기	dry	ache	ambulance	cheap	boil

1 ____________ : to feel pain in your body

2 ____________ : not wet and having no water

3 ____________ : to heat water or soup until it gets very hot

4 ____________ : to pay less for something you buy

5 ____________ : a car used to carry sick people to the hospital

C 다음 단어의 관계가 A:B=C:D가 되도록 알맞은 단어를 골라 빈 칸에 적으세요.

1 clothes : jeans = ______________ : cow

① actor ② pig ③ animal
④ fruit ⑤ milk

2 ______________: together = always : never

① alone ② able ③ study
④ dirty ⑤ usually

3 draw : ______________ = eat : breakfast

① above ② clean ③ photo
④ space ⑤ cartoon

4 red : ______________ = blue : sky

① reded ② apple ③ green
④ snow ⑤ color

5 inside : ______________ = clean : dirty

① space ② angry ③ room
④ outside ⑤ astronaut

D 문맥에 맞게 다음 문장을 완성하세요.

1 They stayed warm by •	• a burning firewood.
2 Would you like to •	• b flying above the Alps.
3 They are milking •	• c eat some grapes?
4 The plane is •	• d about wild animals.
5 I read a book •	• e the cows.

E 문장을 읽고 문맥에 적절한 단어를 고르세요.

1 Minsu (drew/cleaned) a cartoon about a mouse and a cat.

2 The (ambulance/station) carried my mother to the hospital.

3 Tim wants to be an (astronaut/actor) for action movies.

4 Yuna is (drying/drawing) her hair with a towel.

5 Jimin (eats/cleans) breakfast as soon as she gets up.

F 문장의 빈칸에 알맞은 단어를 〈보기〉에서 찾아 쓰세요. (필요하면 형태를 고치세요.)

보기 teach space sky cheap jeans

1 My father ____________ math at school.
우리 아빠는 학교에서 수학을 가르치신다.

2 Jinsu bought good books at ____________ prices.
진수는 좋은 책들을 싼 가격에 구입했다.

3 The rainbow hangs in the ____________.
하늘에 무지개가 떠 있다.

4 Dad bought a new pair of ____________ for me.
아빠가 새 청바지 한 벌을 사 주셨다.

5 We can travel in ____________ in near future.
우리는 가까운 장래에 우주에서 여행을 할 수 있을 것이다.

G 그림에 해당하는 낱말을 〈보기〉에서 골라 쓰세요.

1

(   )

2

(   )

3

(   )

4

(   )

5

(   )

6

(   )

보기 astronaut boil eat act ache wet

Study More

about의 다양한 쓰임

- [be about to+동사] : '(곧) ~하려고 하다'
  We **are about to** leave. 우리는 막 떠나려고 한다.
- 시간, 수량 등과 함께 쓰여서 '대략'의 뜻을 나타낸다.
  Subin walked **about** one hour to the new library. 수빈이는 새 도서관까지 약 1시간을 걸었다.

Day 03

MP3

041 **club** [klʌb]

명 동아리, 동호회

a tennis club 테니스 동호회
president of a discussion club 토론 동아리 회장

042 **join** [dʒɔin]

동 가입하다 join-joined-joined

join a dance class 댄스교실에 등록하다
join a basketball club 농구 동아리에 가입하다

043 **call** [kɔːl]

동 부르다, 전화하다 call-called-called

call the police 경찰에게 전화하다
call him Eric 그를 Eric이라고 부르다

044 **phone** [foun]

명 전화

answer the phone 전화를 받다
hang up the phone 전화를 끊다

045 **easy** [íːzi]

형 쉬운

an easy question 쉬운 질문 an easy story 쉬운 이야기

046 **difficult** [dífəkʌ̀lt]

형 어려운

difficult problems 어려운 문제들 a difficult job 어려운 일

047 **morning** [mɔ́ːrniŋ]

명 아침

in the morning 아침에 Good morning! 좋은 아침!

048 **night** [nait]

명 밤

at night 밤에 on Friday night 금요일 밤

049 **end** [end]

명 끝 동 끝나다 end-ended-ended

end a party 파티를 끝내다
the end of the story 이 이야기의 끝

050 **begin** [bigín]

동 시작하다 begin-began-begun

begin to cry 울기 시작하다
begin a new life 새로운 삶을 시작하다

Daily Test

| 월 일 |

A 우리말에 맞게 빈 칸에 알맞은 단어를 쓰세요.

1 I'm a member of the reading ______________. 나는 독서 동아리의 일원이다.

2 Why don't you ______________ us on our trip to Tokyo? 우리랑 도쿄여행에 함께 가는 건 어때?

3 John ______________ his daughter 'princess'. John은 그녀의 딸을 공주님이라 불렀다.

4 May I use your ______________? 전화를 좀 써도 될까요?

5 This activity looks ______________ and fun. 이 활동은 쉽고 재미있어 보인다.

6 This book is too ______________ for me to understand. 이 책은 내가 이해하기에 너무 어렵다.

7 I usually play tennis in the ______________. 나는 아침에 대개 테니스를 친다.

8 Max couldn't sleep last ______________. Max는 지난 밤 잠을 잘 수 없었다.

9 We'll go to Japan at the ______________ of this month. 우리는 이번 달 말에 일본에 갈 것이다.

10 The baby ______________ to cry. 아기가 울기 시작했다.

B 빈 칸에 알맞은 단어를 고르세요.

1 There will be a party for Tim tomorrow. Can you ______________ us?
① join ② speak ③ end ④ afford ⑤ easy

2 The math exam was quite ______________.
① end ② call ③ age ④ difficult ⑤ address

3 Let's ______________ to clean the house.
① ankle ② easy ③ join ④ noodle ⑤ begin

Day 03

MP3

051 **happy** [hǽpi]

형 행복한

a happy smile 행복한 미소　look happy 행복해 보이다

052 **bird** [bəːrd]

명 새

a small bird 작은 새　a bird's nest 새의 둥지

053 **rabbit** [rǽbit]

명 토끼

a white rabbit 흰 토끼　run like a rabbit 토끼처럼 뛰다

054 **noodle** [núːdl]

명 국수

rice or noodles 밥 또는 국수
chicken noodle soup 닭고기 국수

055 **address** [ədrés]

명 주소

school address 학교 주소
Jina's email address Jina의 이메일 주소

056 **afford** [əfɔ́ːrd]

동 여유가 있다

afford to+**동사원형** ~할 여유가 있다
can't afford a car 자동차를 가질 여유가 없다

057 **afraid** [əfréid]

형 두려운

be afraid of dogs 강아지를 두려워하다
be afraid of darkness 어둠을 두려워하다

058 **again** [əgén]

부 다시

See you again. 다시 만나자.　again and again 되풀이하여

059 **age** [eidʒ]

명 나이

at the age of 16 16살의 나이　at an early age 이른 나이에

060 **ankle** [ǽŋkl]

명 발목

move my ankle 발목을 움직이다　twist my ankle 발목을 접지르다

Daily Test

| 월 일 |

A 우리말에 맞게 빈 칸에 알맞은 단어를 쓰세요.

1 I'm very ______________ for you. 당신 덕분에 정말 행복해요.

2 A ______________ has wings and feathers. 새는 날개와 깃털을 가지고 있다.

3 A ______________ has long ears. 토끼는 긴 귀를 가지고 있다.

4 Chicken ______________ soup is Kate's favorite dish.
닭고기 국수는 Kate의 가장 좋아하는 음식이다.

5 What's your name and ______________? 당신의 이름과 주소는 무엇입니까?

6 I can't ______________ a car. 나는 자동차를 가질 여유가 없다.

7 My sister is ______________ of dogs. 내 여동생은 개를 무서워한다.

8 When will we see Jane ______________? 우리는 Jane과 언제 다시 만날까요?

9 He won his first race at the ______________ of 16.
그는 16살의 나이에 그의 첫 경주에서 우승했다.

10 I can't bend my ______________. 나는 발목을 구부릴 수 없다.

B 빈 칸에 알맞은 단어를 고르세요.

1 I'm ______________ of sleeping alone.
① afraid ② again ③ afford ④ begin ⑤ noodle

2 She got a Nobel prize at the ______________ of 30.
① noodle ② ankle ③ age ④ afraid ⑤ space

3 Peter couldn't remember his ______________.
① night ② address ③ afraid ④ phone ⑤ ankle

Day 04

MP3

061 **left** [left]

형 왼쪽의 부 왼쪽에, 왼쪽으로

the left arm 왼팔 turn left 좌회전 하다

062 **radio** [réidiòu]

명 라디오

listen to the radio 라디오를 듣다
a radio program 라디오 프로그램

063 **big** [big]

형 큰 big - bigger - biggest

a big problem 큰 문제 a big tree 큰 나무

064 **salt** [sɔːlt]

명 소금

salt water 소금물 pass the salt 소금을 건네다

065 **listen** [lísn]

동 듣다 listen - listened - listened

listen to music 음악을 듣다 listen to a speech 연설을 듣다

066 **math** [mæθ]

명 수학

study math 수학을 공부하다 be good at math 수학을 잘하다

067 **make** [meik]

동 만들다 make - made - made

make money 돈을 벌다 make a fire 불을 지피다

068 **cake** [keik]

명 케이크

a birthday cake 생일 케이크 bake a cake 케이크를 굽다

069 **kite** [kait]

명 연

fly a kite 연을 날리다 make a kite 연을 만들다

070 **fly** [flai]

동 날다, 날리다 fly - flew - flown

fly in the sky 하늘을 날다
fly a model airplane 모형 비행기를 날리다

Daily Test

| 월 일 |

A 우리말에 맞게 빈 칸에 알맞은 단어를 쓰세요.

1 Go straight and turn ______________. 직진 하셔서 좌회전 하세요.

2 Do you listen to the ______________ every night? 매일 저녁마다 라디오를 듣나요?

3 There is a ______________ apple tree in Amy's garden.
Amy의 정원에는 큰 사과 나무가 있다.

4 Pass me the ______________, please. 소금 좀 건네주세요.

5 ______________ carefully to what the teacher says.
선생님이 하시는 말들을 주의깊게 들어라.

6 I have ______________ class on Tuesdays. 화요일마다 수학 수업이 있다.

7 Do you want to ______________ a pumpkin pie? 너는 호박파이를 만들고 싶니?

8 We baked a chocolate ______________ for Larry's birthday.
우리는 Larry의 생일을 위해 초콜릿 케이크를 구웠다.

9 We went to the park to fly a ______________. 우리는 연을 날리러 공원에 갔다.

10 Susan's balloon ______________ away in the wind.
Susan은 풍선은 바람에 날려갔다.

B 빈 칸에 알맞은 단어를 고르세요.

1 There are three ______________ apples on the table.
① fly ② big ③ ahead ④ right ⑤ sun

2 My hobby is to ______________ cookies.
① small ② safe ③ make ④ ago ⑤ listen

3 Some people are ______________ to music on the bus.
① listening ② making ③ left ④ aheading ⑤ finishing

Day 04

MP3

071 guitar [gitáːr]

명 기타

play the guitar 기타를 연주하다
buy a new guitar 새 기타를 사다

072 room [ru(ː)m]

명 방

a guest room 손님용 방 enter a room 방에 들어가다

073 invent [invént]

동 발명하다 invent-invented-invented 명 invention 발명

invent the car 자동차를 발명하다
invent the telephone 전화기를 발명하다

074 right [rait]

형 오른쪽의 부 오른쪽으로, 우측으로

the right hand 오른쪽 손
Turn right at the corner. 길 모퉁이에서 오른쪽으로 도세요.

075 small [smɔːl]

형 작은 small-smaller-smallest

a small house 작은 집 a small car 작은 차

076 music [mjúːzik]

명 음악

music class 음악 수업 rock music 락 음악

077 ago [əgóu]

부 ~전에

3 years ago 3년 전에 a long time ago 오래 전에

078 ahead [əhéd]

부 앞으로, 앞에

run ahead 앞으로 달려가다
Go straight ahead. 앞으로 똑바로 가세요.

079 almost [ɔ́ːlmoust]

부 거의

almost all 거의 전부 almost every day 거의 매일

080 already [ɔːlrédi]

부 이미

already know the answer 이미 답을 알다
already finished homework 이미 숙제를 끝냈다

Daily Test

| 월 일 |

A 우리말에 맞게 빈 칸에 알맞은 단어를 쓰세요.

1 Can Seho play the ______________? 세호는 기타를 연주할 줄 아니?

2 The ______________ was dark and cold. 방은 어둡고 추웠다.

3 Who ______________ the camera? 누가 카메라를 발명했나요?

4 Put your ______________ hand up. 당신의 오른손을 드세요.

5 The next room is too ______________. 옆 방은 너무 작다.

6 Helen's hobby is listening to ______________. Helen의 취미는 음악 듣기 이다.

7 He made these toys a long time ______________.
그는 오래 전에 이 장난감들을 만들었다.

8 Tim is looking straight ______________. Tim은 앞을 똑바로 보고 있다.

9 That car ______________ hit me. 거의 차에 치일 뻔 했다.

10 She ______________ arrived at home. 그녀는 이미 집에 도착했다.

B 빈 칸에 알맞은 단어를 고르세요.

1 Who ______________ the phone?
① invented ② ahead ③ already ④ room ⑤ away

2 It's a ______________ world.
① room ② small ③ ahead ④ almost ⑤ ago

3 I'll run ______________ and get some help.
① ago ② room ③ before ④ ahead ⑤ fly

Review Test 02

Day 03 + Day 04 | 월 일 |

A 우리말에 맞게 빈 칸에 알맞은 단어를 쓰세요.

1 ________________ the police 경찰에게 전화하다

2 the ________________ of the story 이 이야기의 끝

3 Jina's email ________________ Jina의 이메일 주소

4 can't ________________ a car 자동차를 가질 여유가 없다

5 be ________________ of darkness 어둠을 두려워하다

6 on Friday ________________ 금요일 밤

7 ________________ money 돈을 벌다

8 3 years ________________ 3년 전에

9 run ________________ 앞으로 달려가다

10 ________________ every day. 거의 매일

B 다음 영어 풀이에 알맞은 어휘를 〈보기〉에서 고르세요.

보기	bird	club	kite	invent	radio

1 ____________ : a group of people who meet to do an activity together

2 ____________ : a machine you can turn on or listen to

3 ____________ : an animal which has wings and can fly

4 ____________ : to create a useful thing that did not exist before

5 ____________ : a kind of toy you can fly with strings

C 다음 단어의 관계가 A:B=C:D가 되도록 알맞은 단어를 골라 빈 칸에 적으세요.

1 ________________ : club = call : friend

① book ② end ③ join
④ afford ⑤ again

2 light : dark = ________________ : night

① sun ② morning ③ beautiful
④ moon ⑤ good

3 ________________ : inventor = sing : singer

① listen ② play ③ invention
④ almost ⑤ invent

4 ________________ : end = happy : sad

① begin ② afraid ③ big
④ right ⑤ ago

5 enter : ________________ = read : newspaper

① happy ② bird ③ radio
④ room ⑤ club

D 문맥에 맞게 다음 문장을 완성하세요.

1 Go straight and	• •	a turn left.
2 We baked a chocolate cake	• •	b easy and fun.
3 She already	• •	c for Larry's birthday.
4 This activity looks	• •	d see Jane again?
5 When will we	• •	e arrived at home.

E 문장을 읽고 문맥에 적절한 단어를 고르세요.

1 Don't forget to turn the (radio/kite) off when you go to bed.

2 Joe wants to be a member of the reading (room/club).

3 At the (age/phone) of sixteen, he became a famous tennis player.

4 His hands are so (big/right) that he can hold a basketball with one hand.

5 Most children in the village went out to (invent/fly) kites.

F 문장의 빈칸에 알맞은 단어를 〈보기〉에서 찾아 쓰세요. (필요하면 형태를 고치세요.)

보기	small	ankle	noodle	rabbit	bird

1 The small white ____________ started to run toward me.
그 작고 하얀 토끼가 내 쪽으로 뛰어 오기 시작했다.

2 Jinsu took a photo of some little ____________ on a tree.
진수는 나무 위에 있는 어린 새들의 사진을 찍었다.

3 The ____________ baby cried for more milk.
그 작은 아기는 우유를 더 달라고 울었다.

4 My little sister broke her ____________ when playing tennis.
내 여동생은 테니스를 하다 발목이 부러졌다.

5 My father likes to eat ____________ dishes.
우리 아빠는 면 요리를 먹는 것을 좋아하신다.

G 그림과 낱말이 잘못 짝지어진 것을 고르세요. ……………………………………………… (　　　　　)

ⓐ

ankle

ⓑ

difficult

ⓒ

happy

ⓓ

kite

H 낱말과 어울리는 그림을 연결하세요.

1 right •　　　　• ⓐ

2 listening •　　　　• ⓑ

Study More

to를 필요로 하는 동사

- [listen to ~] : '~을 듣다'
  My mother likes to **listen to** the radio when she is cooking. 어머니는 요리 할 때 라디오를 듣는다.
- [afford to ~] : '~할 여유가 된다'
  We cannot **afford to** spend any more money on furniture. 우리는 더 이상 가구에 돈을 쓸 여유가 없다.
  The man **can afford** to help the poor. 그 남자는 가난한 사람들을 도와줄 돈을 쓸 여유가 된다.

Day 05

MP3

081 ☐ **before** [bifɔ́ːr]

전 ~전에

before lunch 점심 식사 전에 　 before March 13 3월 13일 전에

082 ☐ **boring** [bɔ́ːriŋ]

형 지루한

a boring movie 지루한 영화 　 a boring story 지루한 이야기

083 ☐ **safe** [seif]

형 안전한 　 safe-safer-safest

a safe place 안전한 장소 　 feel safe 안전하게 느끼다

084 ☐ **area** [ɛ́əriə]

명 지역

in this area 이 지역에서 　 a desert area 사막 지역

085 ☐ **food** [fuːd]

명 음식

Korean food 한국 음식 　 junk food 인스턴트 식품

086 ☐ **body** [bádi]

명 몸, 신체

a human body 인체 　 a part of the body 신체의 한 부분

087 ☐ **leg** [leg]

명 다리

frog's legs 개구리 다리 　 break my leg 다리가 부러지다

088 ☐ **sun** [sʌn]

명 태양 　 형 sunny 화창한

the hot sun 뜨거운 태양 　 a sunny day 화창한 날

089 ☐ **away** [əwéi]

부 떨어져, 다른 데로

far away 멀리 떨어진 　 go away 떠나다

090 ☐ **baby** [béibi]

명 아기

baby clothes 아기용 옷 　 a cute baby 귀여운 아기

Daily Test

| 월 일 |

A 우리말에 맞게 빈 칸에 알맞은 단어를 쓰세요.

1 You should finish your homework ______________ Friday.
너는 금요일 전에 숙제를 마쳐야 한다.

2 I think this book is ______________. 이 책은 지루하다.

3 We wish you a ______________ trip. 우리는 너의 여행이 안전하길 바란다.

4 There are a lot of wild animals in this ______________.
이 지역에는 야생 동물들이 많다.

5 Junk ______________ is very bad for humans.
인스턴트 식품은 사람들에게 매우 좋지 않다.

6 Your ______________ is made up of every part of you.
너의 몸은 너의 모든 부분이다.

7 I broke my right ______________. 나는 오른쪽 다리가 부러졌다.

8 Today's weather is ______________. 오늘의 날씨는 맑다.

9 She lives far ______________ from my home.
그녀는 내 집에서 멀리 떨어져 살고 있다.

10 The ______________ is crying. 아기가 울고 있다.

B 빈 칸에 알맞은 단어를 고르세요.

1 This place is one of the coolest ______________ on Earth.
① away ② around ③ bamboo ④ dish ⑤ areas

2 They will go ______________ soon.
① another ② after ③ away ④ dangerous ⑤ safe

3 This movie is too ______________.
① safe ② dish ③ afford ④ boring ⑤ pretty

Day 05

MP3

091 **dish** [diʃ]

명 요리, 접시

a main dish 주 요리　　a nice dish 좋은 음식

092 **band** [bænd]

명 밴드, 악대

a rock band 락 밴드　　the children's band 어린이 밴드

093 **movie** [múːvi]

명 영화

watch a movie 영화를 보다
become a movie director 영화 감독이 되다

094 **foot** [fut]

명 발　　복 feet

on your right foot 오른 발 위에　　on foot 걸어서

095 **dangerous** [déindʒərəs]

형 위험한　dangerous-more dangerous-most dangerous

a dangerous road 위험한 길　　a dangerous sport 위험한 운동

096 **autumn** [ɔ́ːtəm]

명 가을

autumn leaves 단풍　　late autumn 늦가을

097 **sunglasses** [sʌ́nglæ̀siz]

명 선글라스

wear sunglasses 선글라스를 쓰다
a pair of sunglasses 선글라스 한 개

098 **delicious** [dilíʃəs]

형 맛있는

a delicious smell 맛있는 냄새
a delicious dinner 맛있는 저녁 식사

099 **bamboo** [bæmbúː]

명 대나무

a bamboo chair 대나무 의자　　a bamboo basket 대나무 바구니

100 **after** [ǽftər]

전 ~후에

after breakfast 아침 식사 후에　　after an hour 1시간 후에

Daily Test

| 월 일 |

A 우리말에 맞게 빈 칸에 알맞은 단어를 쓰세요.

1 The ______________ was nice and delicious. 음식은 좋았고 맛있었다.

2 I'm a member of the school ______________. 나는 학교 밴드의 일원이다.

3 His dream is to become a famous ______________ director. 그의 꿈은 유명한 영화 감독이 되는 것이다.

4 I sometimes go to school on ______________. 나는 때때로 걸어서 학교에 간다.

5 A tiger is a ______________ animal. 호랑이는 위험한 동물이다.

6 Tree leaves change color in the ______________. 가을에는 나뭇잎의 색깔이 바뀐다.

7 Wendy is wearing ______________. Wendy는 선글라스를 쓰고 있다.

8 It's so ______________. You're a good cook! 맛있군요. 당신은 훌륭한 요리사에요!

9 Father made a ______________ chair. 아버지는 대나무 의자를 만들었다.

10 We'll leave ______________ dinner. 우리는 저녁 식사 후에 떠날 것이다.

B 빈 칸에 알맞은 단어를 고르세요.

1 I'll call you ______________ 2 o'clock.
① after ② baby ③ dangerous ④ away ⑤ brush

2 This place is too ______________.
① movie ② room ③ dangerous ④ foot ⑤ area

3 Kimchi is a ______________ Korean food.
① autumn ② sun ③ bamboo ④ body ⑤ delicious

Day 06

MP3

101 **save** [seiv]

동 절약하다 save-saved-saved

save money 돈을 절약하다 save time 시간을 아끼다

102 **money** [mʌ́ni]

명 돈

a lot of money 많은 돈 spend money 돈을 쓰다

103 **brush** [brʌʃ]

명 빗 동 닦다, 빗다 brush-brushed-brushed

a hairbrush 머리 빗 brush your teeth 이를 닦다

104 **necklace** [néklis]

명 목걸이

a gold necklace 금 목걸이

wear a diamond necklace 다이아몬드 목걸이를 하고 있다

105 **bark** [bá:rk]

동 짖다 명 (개, 동물) 짖는 소리 bark-barked-barked

bark at ~에게 짖어대다 a dog's bark 개 짖는 소리

106 **coat** [kout]

명 코트

a raincoat 우비 a thick coat 두꺼운 코트

107 **jacket** [dʒǽkit]

명 자켓

a sport jacket 스포츠 자켓 wear a jacket 자켓을 입다

108 **seafood** [sí:fù:d]

명 해산물

fresh seafood 신선한 해산물

a seafood restaurant 해산물 식당

109 **pretty** [príti]

형 예쁜 부 꽤, 매우 pretty-prettier-prettiest

a pretty doll 예쁜 인형 a pretty good movie 꽤 좋은 영화

110 **get** [get]

동 타다, 얻다 get-got-gotten

get on the bus 버스에 타다 get a job 일자리를 얻다

Daily Test

| 월 일 |

A 우리말에 맞게 빈 칸에 알맞은 단어를 쓰세요.

1 We have to ______________ energy. 우리는 에너지를 절약해야 한다.

2 We spent a lot of ______________ on clothes. 우리는 옷에 많은 돈을 썼다.

3 Mom ______________ my hair every morning. 엄마는 매일 아침 나의 머리를 빗겨준다.

4 Yuri is wearing a gold ______________. 유리는 금 목걸이를 하고 있다.

5 The dog started to ______________ at him. 그 개는 그를 향해 짖기 시작했다.

6 Jessica is wearing a yellow ______________. Jessica는 노란색 코트를 입고 있다.

7 I bought a sport ______________ yesterday. 나는 어제 스포츠 자켓을 샀다.

8 Fresh ______________ is good for your health. 신선한 해산물은 건강에 좋다.

9 There are many ______________ flowers in the street. 거리에 예쁜 꽃들이 많이 있다.

10 John and I ______________ the first prize in the science contest.
John과 나는 과학 대회에서 1등을 했다.

B 빈 칸에 알맞은 단어를 고르세요.

1 Ann is going to ______________ a new cell phone.
① lose ② get ③ bar ④ back ⑤ pretty

2 I ______________ money to buy a new dress.
① saved ② bath ③ brushed ④ bar ⑤ barber

3 You should ______________ your teeth three times a day.
① lose ② dirty ③ dentist ④ brush ⑤ bath

Day 06

MP3

111 **lose** [luːz]

동 잃다, 지다 lose-lost-lost

lose a wallet 지갑을 잃어버리다 lose a game 경기에서 지다

112 **smart** [smaːrt]

형 똑똑한 smart-smarter-smartest

a smart boy 똑똑한 소년 look smart 똑똑해 보이다

113 **doctor** [dáktər]

명 의사

see a doctor / go to the doctor 병원에 가다

114 **choose** [tʃuːz]

동 선택하다 choose-chose-chosen

choose a book 책을 고르다 choose a dish 음식을 선택하다

115 **dentist** [déntist]

명 치과 의사

see a dentist / go to the dentist 치과에 가다

116 **bar** [baːr]

명 바, 막대

candy bar 사탕 바 a bar of chocolate 초콜릿 한 개

117 **barber** [báːrbər]

명 이발사

a barber shop 이발소 go to the barber 이발소에 가다

118 **ring** [riŋ]

명 반지

wear a ring / put on a ring 반지를 끼다

119 **basket** [bǽskit]

명 바구니

a picnic basket 소풍 바구니 in the basket 바구니 안에

120 **bath** [bæθ]

명 목욕

take a bath / have a bath 목욕을 하다

Daily Test

| 월 일 |

A 우리말에 맞게 빈 칸에 알맞은 단어를 쓰세요.

1 She ____________ her room key. 그녀는 그녀의 방 키를 잃어버렸다.

2 Jimin is handsome and ____________. 지민은 잘생기고 똑똑하다.

3 You look so sick. You should see a ____________.
너는 아파 보이는구나. 병원에 가야겠어.

4 We ____________ Tim as class president. 우리는 Tim을 반장으로 뽑았다.

5 I went to the ____________ last week. 나는 지난 주에 치과에 다녀왔다.

6 This chocolate ____________ has too much sugar in it.
이 초콜릿 바는 속에 너무 많은 설탕이 들어있다.

7 Where is the nearest ____________ shop? 가장 가까운 이발소가 어디에 있습니까?

8 Jieun put a ____________ on her finger. 지은은 그녀의 손가락에 반지를 끼웠다.

9 Many fruits are in the ____________. 바구니 안에 많은 과일들이 있다.

10 My brother usually takes a ____________ before going to bed.
내 남동생은 보통 자러 가기 전에 목욕을 한다.

B 빈 칸에 알맞은 단어를 고르세요.

1 Lisa is a ____________ student.
① get ② ring ③ smart ④ save ⑤ difficult

2 She ____________ a new coat to wear.
① chose ② barber ③ bar ④ saved ⑤ barked

3 It's time to take a ____________.
① lose ② ring ③ bark ④ bath ⑤ brush

Review Test 03

Day 05 + Day 06 | 월 일 |

Ⓐ 우리말에 맞게 빈 칸에 알맞은 단어를 쓰세요.

1 a desert ________________ 사막 지역

2 far ________________ 멀리 떨어진

3 junk ________________ 인스턴트 식품

4 on ________________ 걸어서

5 a ________________ road 위험한 길

6 ________________ money 돈을 절약하다

7 ________________ at ~에게 짖어대다

8 ________________ on the bus 버스에 타다

9 ________________ a wallet 지갑을 잃어버리다

10 ________________ a book 책을 고르다

Ⓑ 다음 영어 풀이에 알맞은 어휘를 〈보기〉에서 고르세요.

보기	delicious	sun	boring	dangerous	bath

1 ____________ : not interesting or exciting

2 ____________ : not safe and likely to harm or hurt you

3 ____________ : to wash your body with water

4 ____________ : a kind of star that gives Earth heat and light

5 ____________ : having a good taste and smell

C 다음 단어의 관계가 A:B=C:D가 되도록 알맞은 단어를 골라 빈 칸에 적으세요.

1 after : before = ________________ : dangerous

① safe ② area ③ away
④ delicious ⑤ fresh

2 save : money = ________________ : hair

① band ② brush ③ movie
④ before ⑤ choose

3 fresh : ________________ = beautiful : flower

① dentist ② ring ③ barber
④ sky ⑤ seafood

4 sun : ________________ = rain : umbrella

① cloud ② dish ③ sunglasses
④ moon ⑤ bark

5 delicious : dish = expensive : ________________

① necklace ② cheap ③ money
④ dollar ⑤ short

D 문맥에 맞게 다음 문장을 완성하세요.

1 His dream is to become •	• a before going to bed.
2 Tree leaves change color •	• b in the autumn.
3 You should finish your homework •	• c a famous movie director.
4 Jessica is wearing •	• d a yellow coat.
5 My brother usually takes a bath •	• e before Friday.

E 문장을 읽고 문맥에 적절한 단어를 고르세요.

1 It is very cold outside. Take your (jacket/sunglasses) with you when you go out.

2 He didn't have enough (basket/money) to buy a new computer.

3 Ted is going to the (barber/dentist) for a haircut.

4 Yumi is going to see the (dentist/band) because she has a toothache.

5 The sky became clear (away/after) the rain stopped.

F 문장의 빈칸에 알맞은 단어를 〈보기〉에서 찾아 쓰세요. (필요하면 형태를 고치세요.)

보기	smart	pretty	bamboo	dish	body

1 She is growing ____________ flowers in her front garden.
그녀는 예쁜 꽃들을 앞 정원에 키우고 있다.

2 Sam exercises every day to keep a healthy ____________.
Sam은 건강한 몸을 유지하기 위해 날마다 운동을 한다.

3 Today's main ____________ is beef steak with tomato sauce.
오늘의 주 요리는 토마토 소스를 곁들인 소고기 스테이크다.

4 This chair is made of ____________ and very comfortable.
이 의자는 대나무로 만들어졌고 아주 편안하다.

5 Jaemin is a ____________ and quiet boy.
재민은 똑똑하고 조용한 소년이다.

G 그림에 해당하는 낱말을 〈보기〉에서 골라 쓰세요.

1 

(   )

2 

(   )

3 

(   )

4 

(   )

5 

(   )

6 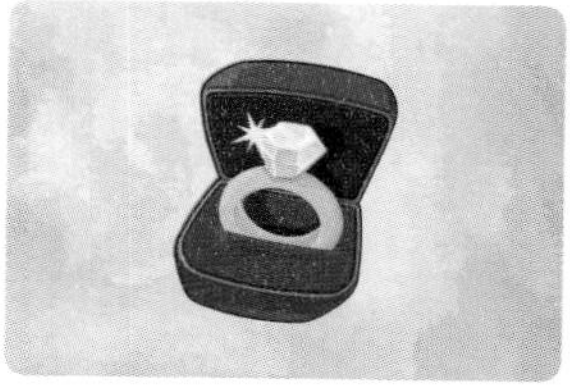

(   )

보기 delicious basket broken boring ring doctor

Study More

비슷한 의미를 가진 before와 in front of

- [before+시간 명사/장소 명사] : ~전에
  You have to finish your homework **before** dinner. 저녁 식사 전에 숙제를 마쳐야 해.
- [in front of+장소 명사] : ~앞에
  There is an old pine tree **in front of** the house. 그 집 앞에는 늙은 소나무 한 그루가 서 있다.

Day 07

MP3

121 **day** [dei]

명 낮, 하루, 날

during the day 낮 동안　　for six days 6일 동안

122 **become** [bikʌ́m]

동 ~이 되다　become - became - become

become a lawyer 변호사가 되다
become a dancer 무용수가 되다

123 **minute** [mainjúːt]

명 분

30 minutes 30분　　for 10 minutes 10분 동안

124 **month** [mʌnθ]

명 달

once a month 한 달에 한 번　　next month 다음 달

125 **king** [kiŋ]

명 왕

the King of England 영국의 왕　　become a king 왕이 되다

126 **pull** [pul]

동 끌다, 잡아 당기다　pull - pulled - pulled

pull a chair 의자를 끌다　　pull a curtain 커튼을 치다

127 **soldier** [sóuldʒər]

명 군인, 병사

young soldiers 어린 군인들　　The Roman soldiers 로마 병사들

128 **princess** [prínsis]

명 공주

a pretty princess 아름다운 공주　　like a princess 공주처럼

129 **push** [puʃ]

동 누르다, 밀다　push - pushed - pushed

push a button 버튼을 누르다　　push a cart 카트를 밀다

130 **bean** [biːn]

명 콩

coffee beans 커피 콩　　small beans 작은 콩들

Daily Test

| 월 일 |

A 우리말에 맞게 빈 칸에 알맞은 단어를 쓰세요.

1 The sun is shining during the ______________. 태양은 낮 동안 빛나고 있다.

2 Susan wants to ______________ a dancer. Susan은 무용수가 되길 원한다.

3 I'll call again in about 10 ______________. 내가 대략 10분 후에 다시 전화 할게요.

4 We will go to LA next ______________. 우리는 다음달에 LA에 갈 것이다.

5 The boy will become the ______________ of England. 그 소년은 영국의 왕이 될 것이다.

6 I'll ______________ the curtains. 내가 커튼을 칠게요.

7 The ______________ quickly hid himself in the bush. 그 군인은 빠르게 덤불 속으로 숨었다.

8 She looks like a ______________. 그녀는 공주처럼 보인다.

9 I ______________ the red button. 나는 빨간 버튼을 눌렀다.

10 I bought some coffee ______________. 나는 약간의 커피 콩을 샀다.

B 빈 칸에 알맞은 단어를 고르세요.

1 She ______________ the doorbell again.
① lost ② pushed ③ beaten ④ became ⑤ barked

2 I'll arrive in about 30 ______________.
① basket ② minutes ③ bars ④ pulls ⑤ beats

3 My brother ______________ a doctor.
① became ② bamboo ③ month ④ flower ⑤ crown

Day 07

MP3

131 **different** [dífərənt]

형 다른

a different idea 다른 생각
three different colors 세 가지 다른 색깔

132 **subject** [sʌ́bdʒikt]

명 과목

a school subject 학교 과목
my favorite subject 내가 가장 좋아하는 과목

133 **science** [sáiəns]

명 과학

study science 과학을 공부하다　a science class 과학 수업

134 **flower** [fláuər]

명 꽃

a beautiful flower 아름다운 꽃　a flower garden 꽃밭

135 **prince** [prins]

명 왕자

The Little Prince 어린 왕자　the Prince of Egypt 이집트 왕자

136 **same** [seim]

부 같은

at the same time 동시에　the same topic 같은 주제

137 **crown** [kraun]

명 왕관

a golden crown 황금 왕관　wear a crown 왕관을 쓰다

138 **beat** [biːt]

동 치다　명 박자　beat-beat-beaten

beat the drums 드럼을 치다　a strong beat 강한 박자

139 **because** [bikɔ́(ː)z]

접 ~때문에

because of a storm 태풍 때문에
Because he was sick. 그가 아팠기 때문이다.

140 **hour** [áuər]

명 시간

8 hours a day 하루 8시간　half an hour 30분

Daily Test

| 월 일 |

A 우리말에 맞게 빈 칸에 알맞은 단어를 쓰세요.

1 These bags are ________________ in size. 이 가방들은 크기가 다르다.

2 What ________________ do you like? 네가 좋아하는 과목은 무엇이니?

3 I like to study ________________. 나는 과학 공부하는 것을 좋아한다.

4 There are many beautiful ________________ in the garden. 정원에 아름다운 꽃들이 많이 있다.

5 He looks like a ________________. 그는 왕자처럼 보인다.

6 Jack and I are in the ________________ class at school. Jack과 나는 학교에서 같은 반이다.

7 The king is wearing a ________________. 왕은 왕관을 쓰고 있다.

8 My mother likes music that has a slow ________________. 어머니는 느린 박자의 음악을 좋아한다.

9 ________________ it's raining so heavily, we can't go on a picnic today. 비가 많이 오기 때문에, 우리는 오늘 소풍을 갈 수 없다.

10 Joan plans to study Chinese for two ________________ a day. Joan은 중국어를 하루 2시간씩 공부 할 계획이다.

B 빈 칸에 알맞은 단어를 고르세요.

1 She looks ________________ in her new shirt.
① difficult ② beat ③ subject ④ princess ⑤ different

2 Mike and I go to the ________________ school.
① crown ② minute ③ day ④ same ⑤ subject

3 Ken was late ________________ his car broke down.
① because ② become ③ push ④ pull ⑤ bean

Day 08

MP3

141 **fix** [fiks]

동 고치다 fix-fixed-fixed

fix a machine 기계를 수리하다 fix a car 차를 고치다

142 **useful** [júːsfəl]

형 유용한

useful information 유용한 정보 useful advice 유용한 충고

143 **box** [bɑks]

명 상자

a big box 큰 상자 a jewelry box 보석 상자

144 **hobby** [hɑ́bi]

명 취미

my hobby 나의 취미 a new hobby 새로운 취미

145 **fresh** [freʃ]

형 신선한 fresh-fresher-freshest

fresh fruits 신선한 과일 fresh milk 신선한 우유

146 **air** [εər]

명 공기

into the air 공중으로 night air 밤공기

147 **open** [óupən]

동 열다 형 열린 open-opened-opened

open the door 문을 열다 an open window 열린 창문

148 **cloudy** [kláudi]

형 흐린

a cloudy sky 구름 낀 하늘 cloudy weather 흐린 날씨

149 **purple** [pə́ːrpl]

명 보라색 형 보라색의

a purple flower 보라색 꽃 a purple skirt 보라색 치마

150 **vegetable** [védʒitəbl]

명 야채

fresh vegetables 신선한 야채 vegetable soup 야채 수프

Daily Test

| 월 일 |

A 우리말에 맞게 빈 칸에 알맞은 단어를 쓰세요.

1 Father __________ the bike yesterday. 아버지는 어제 자전거를 고치셨다.

2 We found a lot of __________ information in this book.
우리는 이 책에서 유용한 정보를 많이 찾았다.

3 There is a jewelry __________ on the sofa. 소파 위에 보석 상자가 있다.

4 What's your __________? 당신의 취미는 무엇인가요?

5 I want to eat __________ seafood. 난 신선한 해산물이 먹고 싶다.

6 When you are tired, go out and get some fresh __________!
네가 지칠 때는 밖에 나가서 신선한 공기를 마셔라!

7 Please, __________ the door. 문 좀 열어주세요.

8 Today's weather is __________. 오늘의 날씨는 흐리다.

9 __________ is my favorite color. 보라색은 내가 가장 좋아하는 색이다.

10 My son doesn't like to eat __________ pizza.
내 아들은 야채 피자를 먹기 싫어한다.

B 빈 칸에 알맞은 단어를 고르세요.

1 I __________ my sister's watch.
① board ② box ③ open ④ fixed ⑤ useful

2 This book is very __________ for your study.
① bed ② between ③ air ④ useful ⑤ ride

3 Sam __________ the window to let some fresh air in.
① opened ② rode ③ made ④ barked ⑤ same

Day 08

MP3

151 **use** [ju:s]

동 사용하다 use-used-used

use chopsticks 젓가락을 사용하다
use a computer 컴퓨터를 사용하다

152 **favorite** [féivərit]

형 가장 좋아하는

my favorite season 내가 좋아하는 계절
his favorite time of the year 일년 중 그가 가장 좋아하는 때

153 **help** [help]

명 도움 동 돕다 help-helped-helped

May I help you? 무엇을 도와드릴까요?
help to make a dress 드레스 만드는 것을 돕다

154 **bed** [bed]

명 침대

a single bed 1인용 침대 go to bed 자러 가다

155 **bell** [bel]

명 종

ring a bell 종을 울리다 a doorbell 초인종

156 **between** [bitwí:n]

전 ~사이에

between A and B A와 B 사이에
between Peter and Julian Peter와 Julian 사이에

157 **board** [bɔ:rd]

명 판, 게시판

a diving board 다이빙 판 a notice board 게시판

158 **boat** [bout]

명 배

a fishing boat 낚시 배 take a boat 배를 타다

159 **bone** [boun]

명 뼈

a leg bone 무릎 뼈 animal bones 동물 뼈

160 **ride** [raid]

동 타다 ride-rode-ridden

ride a bus 버스를 타다 ride a horse 말을 타다

Daily Test

| 월 일 |

A 우리말에 맞게 빈 칸에 알맞은 단어를 쓰세요.

1 You can ______________ this dictionary if you want to study Japanese. 일본어를 공부하고 싶으면 이 사전을 이용하면 된다.

2 What's your ______________ movie? 네가 가장 좋아하는 영화는 무엇이니?

3 I ______________ my mom make dinner. 나는 엄마가 저녁 준비하는 것을 도와 드렸다.

4 It's time to go to ______________. 자러 갈 시간이다.

5 The teacher rang the ______________ to call the students. 선생님은 학생들을 부르기 위해 종을 쳤다.

6 The restaurant is ______________ the hospital and the park. 식당은 병원과 공원 사이에 있다.

7 The students are looking at the ______________. 학생들은 게시판을 보고 있는 중이다.

8 An empty ______________ is floating on the river. 강 위에 빈 배가 떠 있다.

9 I wonder why dogs like ______________ so much. 나는 개들이 뼈를 왜 그렇게 좋아하는지 궁금하다.

10 Tina wants to ______________ the roller coaster. Tina는 롤러코스터를 타고 싶다.

B 빈 칸에 알맞은 단어를 고르세요.

1 Joe ______________ his mom clean the house.
① helped ② favorite ③ between ④ went ⑤ saw

2 My ______________ color is yellow.
① cloudy ② hate ③ fresh ④ favorite ⑤ useful

3 There is a tower ______________ the two buildings.
① open ② between ③ different ④ beat ⑤ crown

Review Test 04

Day 07 + Day 08 | 월 일 |

A 우리말에 맞게 빈 칸에 알맞은 단어를 쓰세요.

1 ________________ a lawyer 변호사가 되다

2 once a ________________ 한 달에 한 번

3 three ________________ colors 세 가지 다른 색깔

4 the ________________ topic 같은 주제

5 ________________ he was sick. 그가 아팠기 때문이다.

6 ________________ a machine 기계를 수리하다

7 ________________ advice 유용한 충고

8 fresh ________________ 신선한 야채

9 ________________ Peter and Julian Peter와 Julian 사이에

10 small ________________ 작은 콩들

B 다음 영어 풀이에 알맞은 어휘를 〈보기〉에서 고르세요.

보기	ride	pull	beat	push	fresh

1 ____________ : to hold and move something toward you

2 ____________ : to hit something again and again

3 ____________ : to sit on the back of something and control its movement

4 ____________ : newly made, picked, or produced

5 ____________ : to hold and move something away from you

C 다음 단어의 관계가 A:B=C:D가 되도록 알맞은 단어를 골라 빈 칸에 적으세요.

1 long : short = sunny : ______________

① cloudy ② day ③ flower
④ same ⑤ air

2 use : useful = ______________ : helpful

① helped ② helping ③ help
④ helps ⑤ helper

3 ______________ : close = same : different

① opening ② door ③ opened
④ window ⑤ open

4 ______________ : science = flower : rose

① bell ② subject ③ English
④ bed ⑤ math

5 prince : ______________ = lady : gentleman

① king ② board ③ girl
④ princess ⑤ woman

D 문맥에 맞게 다음 문장을 완성하세요.

1	I'll call again	a	fresh seafood.
2	The boy will become	b	in about 10 minutes.
3	Joan plans to study Chinese	c	for two hours a day.
4	I want to eat	d	the King of England.
5	The students are	e	looking at the notice board.

E 문장을 읽고 문맥에 적절한 단어를 고르세요.

1 It is very hot today. Becky, can you (open/beat) the window for me?

2 She went to (bed/box) early because she felt very tired.

3 Please put the old books into this plastic (bean/box).

4 (Use/Beat) this dictionary if you want to study Chinese.

5 He threw the ball into the (day/air) as high as he could.

F 문장의 빈칸에 알맞은 단어를 〈보기〉에서 찾아 쓰세요. (필요하면 형태를 고치세요.)

보기	hobby	beat	favorite	bean	bell

1 The angry man ____________ the table and began to shout.
화가 난 남자는 탁자를 쳤고, 소리치기 시작했다.

2 Soyoung's ____________ school subject is history.
소영이 가장 좋아하는 교과목은 역사다.

3 Unlike its name, the peanut is actually a kind of ____________, not a nut.
이름과 달리 땅콩은 콩의 한 종류이며 견과류는 아니다.

4 Joan's ____________ is cooking.
Joan의 취미는 요리다.

5 The visitor to the house ringed the ____________ and waited.
그 집의 방문자는 초인종을 누르고 기다렸다.

G 그림과 낱말이 잘못 짝지어진 것을 고르세요. .... (   )

ⓐ

fresh

ⓑ

pull

ⓒ

push

ⓓ

soldier

H 낱말과 어울리는 그림을 연결하세요.

1 ride •

2 boat •

• ⓐ 

• ⓑ 

Study More

fix의 다양한 의미

- '~을 고치다/수정하다'
  Dad **fixed** my bike yesterday. 아빠는 어제 내 자전거를 고쳐 주셨다.
- '(장소/날짜 등)을 정하다/잡다'
  Why don't we **fix** a date for the next meeting now? 지금 다음 모임 날짜를 정하는 것이 어때?

Day 09

MP3

161 **art** [ɑːrt]

명 미술, 예술

an art festival 미술 축제　　an art gallery 미술관

162 **write** [rait]

동 쓰다　write-wrote-written

write a letter 편지를 쓰다　　write a book 책을 쓰다

163 **buy** [bai]

동 사다　buy-bought-bought

buy a computer 컴퓨터를 사다　　buy a new bike 새 자전거를 사다

164 **brain** [brein]

명 두뇌, 머리

brain activity 두뇌 활동　　have a good brain 좋은 머리를 가지다

165 **sing** [siŋ]

동 노래하다　sing-sang-sung

sing a song 노래를 부르다　　sing together 함께 노래하다

166 **play** [plei]

동 놀다, 게임을 하다, 연주하다　play-played-played

play with friends 친구들과 놀다　　play soccer 축구를 하다

167 **break** [breik]

명 휴식　동 깨다　break-broke-broken

take a break 휴식을 취하다　　break a window 창문을 깨다

168 **plant** [plænt]

명 식물　동 심다　plant-planted-planted

grow plants 식물을 키우다
plant trees in a garden 정원에 나무를 심다

169 **bridge** [bridʒ]

명 다리

cross a bridge 다리를 건너다
a bridge over a river 강 위의 다리

170 **sorry** [sɔ́(ː)ri]

형 미안한

feel sorry 미안함을 느끼다　　I'm sorry. 미안합니다.

Daily Test

| 월 일 |

A 우리말에 맞게 빈 칸에 알맞은 단어를 쓰세요.

1 My family went to an ______________ festival last week. 우리 가족은 지난 주에 미술 축제에 다녀왔다.

2 Jane ______________ a letter to Jack yesterday. Jane은 어제 Jack에게 편지를 썼다.

3 Jina ______________ a skirt yesterday. Jina는 어제 치마를 샀다.

4 Each side of the ______________ has different functions. 두뇌의 양쪽은 다른 기능을 가지고 있다.

5 Let's ______________ a song together. 함께 노래 부르자.

6 Jamie ______________ soccer with his friends every Saturday. Jamie는 매주 토요일 친구들과 축구를 한다.

7 The camera is ______________ again. 그 카메라는 다시 고장났다.

8 Harry is ______________ a tree in his garden. Harry는 그의 정원에 나무를 심고 있다.

9 The ______________ was built 150 years ago. 그 다리는 150년 전에 지어졌다.

10 I'm ______________, but I can't go to the party. 미안하지만, 난 그 파티에 갈 수 없어.

B 빈 칸에 알맞은 단어를 고르세요.

1 Minsu ______________ the violin in his room.

① played ② card ③ thank ④ artist ⑤ wrote

2 There are lots of ______________ in the garden.

① arts ② plants ③ hobbies ④ games ⑤ brains

3 Tommy ______________ a new drawing book.

① writing ② breathed ③ thanked ④ bought ⑤ sang

Day 09

MP3

171 **future** [fjúːtʃər]

명 미래

in the future 미래에　　future generations 미래 세대

172 **wash** [wɑʃ]

동 씻다　wash-washed-washed

wash your hands 손을 씻다　　wash the dishes 설거지 하다

173 **queen** [kwiːn]

명 여왕, 여신

kings and queens 왕과 여왕　　a kind queen 친절한 여왕

174 **card** [kɑːrd]

명 카드

a Christmas card 크리스마스 카드　　send a card 카드를 보내다

175 **ticket** [tíkit]

명 표

a movie ticket 영화 표　　a one-way ticket 편도 차표

176 **brand** [brænd]

명 브랜드, 상표

a brand name 브랜드 이름　　a brand label 상표 라벨

177 **game** [geim]

명 게임

play a game 게임을 하다　　win a game 게임에서 이기다

178 **breathe** [briːð]

동 숨쉬다　breathe-breathed-breathed

breathe deeply 깊게 숨을 쉬다　　breathe in 숨을 들이쉬다

179 **thank** [θæŋk]

명 감사　동 감사하다　thank-thanked-thanked

thank him for his help 그의 도움에 감사하다
Thank you very much. 정말 감사합니다.

180 **artist** [áːrtist]

명 예술가

a great artist 위대한 예술가　　a professional artist 전문 예술가

Daily Test

| 월 일 |

A 우리말에 맞게 빈 칸에 알맞은 단어를 쓰세요.

1 What do you want to be in the ______________? 당신은 커서 무엇이 되고 싶나요?

2 Father ______________ his car. 아버지는 그의 차를 닦았다.

3 The ______________ is wearing a crown. 여왕은 왕관을 쓰고 있다.

4 Minji sent a ______________ to her grandparents.
민지는 그녀의 조부모님께 크리스마스 카드를 보냈다.

5 Paul has ______________ for the baseball game on Saturday.
Paul은 토요일 야구 게임의 표가 있다.

6 I don't know the bag's ______________ name. 나는 그 가방의 상표 이름을 모른다.

7 Why don't we play a ______________ together? 다같이 게임 하는 건 어때?

8 Mother said, "Tommy, relax and ______________ deeply."
어머니는 "Tommy, 침착하고 숨을 깊게 쉬어"라고 말씀하셨다.

9 ______________ you very much for your time. 시간 내주셔서 정말 감사합니다.

10 My mother is a make-up ______________. 엄마는 메이크업 아티스트이다.

B 빈 칸에 알맞은 단어를 고르세요.

1 James wants to become a scientist in the ______________.
① future ② tickets ③ today ④ week ⑤ last

2 ______________ you for your letter.
① Ticket ② Thank ③ Game ④ Buy ⑤ Break

3 When she is angry, she tries to ______________ deeply.
① brands ② future ③ sorry ④ sings ⑤ breathe

Day 10

MP3

181 **watch** [watʃ]

동 보다 watch-watched-watched

watch TV TV를 보다 watch a movie 영화를 보다

182 **visit** [vízit]

동 방문하다 visit-visited-visited

visit Seoul 서울을 방문하다

visit a friend in Tokyo 도쿄에 있는 친구를 방문하다

183 **grandparents** [grænperənts]

명 조부모

my friendly grandparents 나의 친절한 조부모님

live with her grandparents 그녀의 조부모님과 살다

184 **hungry** [hʌ́ŋgri]

형 배고픈 hungry-hungrier-hungriest

feel hungry 배가 고프다 a hungry boy 배가 고픈 소년

185 **full** [ful]

형 가득한, 배가 부른 full-fuller-fullest

be full 배가 부르다 be full of flowers 꽃으로 가득 차다

186 **thick** [θik]

형 두꺼운 thick-thicker-thickest

a thick book 두꺼운 책 a thick forest 울창한 숲

187 **thin** [θin]

형 얇은 thin-thinner-thinnest

a thin line 얇은 선 thin legs 마른 다리

188 **family** [fǽməli]

명 가족

my family 우리 가족 a happy family 행복한 가족

189 **cousin** [kʌ́zən]

명 사촌

my cousin 내 사촌

a letter from my cousin 사촌으로부터의 편지

190 **mix** [miks]

동 섞다 mix-mixed-mixed

mix butter and sugar 버터와 설탕을 섞다

mix blue and yellow paints 파란색과 노란색 물감을 섞다

Daily Test

| 월 일 |

A 우리말에 맞게 빈 칸에 알맞은 단어를 쓰세요.

1 These days Jack ________________ TV until the late night.
요즘 Jack은 TV를 늦은 시간까지 본다.

2 I ________________ the new City Library last week.
나는 지난주에 새 시립 도서관을 방문했다.

3 Ron lives with his ________________. Ron은 그의 조부모님과 산다.

4 I'm really ________________ now. 나는 지금 매우 배가 고프다.

5 His room is ________________ of dust. 그의 방은 먼지로 가득했다.

6 The book is very ________________. 이 책은 매우 두껍다.

7 Mike is tall and ________________. Mike는 키가 크고 말랐다.

8 What are your ________________ members doing? 너희 가족들은 무엇을 하고 있니?

9 My younger ________________, Tom, is good at dancing.
내 사촌동생 Tom은 춤을 잘 춘다.

10 ________________ butter and sugar in the bowl. 그릇에 버터와 설탕을 섞으세요.

B 빈 칸에 알맞은 단어를 고르세요.

1 Ken is ________________ his daughter's house.
① flying ② mixing ③ falling ④ fulling ⑤ visiting

2 This book is too ________________ to carry.
① full ② mix ③ thick ④ dead ⑤ watch

3 Teachers and students ________________ the football game together.
① sport ② dead ③ mixed ④ watched ⑤ visiting

Day 10

MP3

191 **season** [síːzən]

명 계절

four seasons 사계절　a rainy season 우기

192 **fall** [fɔːl]

동 떨어지다 명 가을 fall-fell-fallen

fall off the tree 나무에서 떨어지다　in fall 가을에

193 **sport** [spɔːrt]

명 운동

play sports 운동 하다　a team sport 단체 운동

194 **football** [fútbɔ̀ːl]

명 미식 축구

a football game 미식 축구 경기　play football 미식 축구를 하다

195 **carry** [kǽri]

동 옮기다, 휴대하다 carry-carried-carried

carry a pen 펜을 가지고 다니다
carry a suitcase 여행가방을 들고 있다

196 **nurse** [nəːrs]

명 간호사

a hospital nurse 병원 간호사　become a nurse 간호사가 되다

197 **camera** [kǽmərə]

명 카메라

buy a camera 카메라를 사다　fix a camera 카메라를 고치다

198 **dead** [ded]

형 죽은

a dead animal 죽은 동물　dead trees 죽은 나무들

199 **business** [bíznis]

명 사업

a business trip 출장　a family business 가족 사업

200 **butter** [bʌ́tər]

명 버터

spread butter 버터를 펴 바르다　a piece of butter 버터 한 조각

Daily Test

| 월 일 |

A 우리말에 맞게 빈 칸에 알맞은 단어를 쓰세요.

1 We have four ______________ in Korea. 한국은 4계절이 있다.

2 The leaves of the old tree are beginning to ______________.
그 늙은 나무의 잎들이 떨어지기 시작했다.

3 My sister will join a winter ______________ camp next week.
내 여동생은 다음주에 겨울 스포츠 캠프에 참여할 것이다.

4 Playing ______________ is really exciting. 미식 축구를 하는 것은 정말 재미있다.

5 She was ______________ a box. 그녀는 박스를 옮기는 중이었다.

6 Cindy finally became a hospital ______________. Cindy는 마침내 병원 간호사가 되었다.

7 Grandfather gave me a new ______________. 할아버지가 새 카메라를 주셨다.

8 We saw many ______________ trees in the park.
우리는 공원에서 죽은 나무들을 많이 보았다.

9 I will go on a ______________ trip to LA next week.
나는 다음주에 LA로 출장을 갈 것이다.

10 "Nick, spread some ______________ on your toast."
"Nick, 토스트에 버터를 발라보렴."

B 빈 칸에 알맞은 단어를 고르세요.

1 Can you ______________ this box to the bus stop for us?
① carry ② nurse ③ fall ④ dead ⑤ thick

2 People wear a raincoat during the rainy ______________.
① season ② nurse ③ camera ④ brand ⑤ business

3 Father went on a ______________ trip to China last week.
① took ② thick ③ full ④ business ⑤ cousin

Review Test 05

Day 09 + Day 10 | 월 일 |

A 우리말에 맞게 빈 칸에 알맞은 단어를 쓰세요.

1 ________________ together 함께 노래 부르다

2 ________________ generations 미래 세대

3 take a ________________ 휴식을 취하다

4 play ________________ 미식축구를 하다

5 ________________ deeply 깊게 숨을 쉬다

6 ________________ a movie 영화를 보다

7 a kind ________________ 친절한 여왕

8 ________________ butter and sugar 버터와 설탕을 섞다

9 ________________ off the tree 나무에서 떨어지다

10 ________________ a pen 펜을 갖고 있다

B 다음 영어 풀이에 알맞은 어휘를 〈보기〉에서 고르세요.

보기	plant	bridge	nurse	breathe	queen

1 ____________ : to take air into your body and let it out again

2 ____________ : a person who takes care of sick people

3 ____________ : a woman who rules or controls a country

4 ____________ : something that is built to let people or cars cross over a river

5 ____________ : a living thing that grows in soil, and needs water and sunlight

C 다음 단어의 관계가 A:B=C:D가 되도록 알맞은 단어를 골라 빈 칸에 적으세요.

1 art : ________________ = book : writer

① artist ② player ③ singer
④ dancer ⑤ fighter

2 ________________ : ticket = sing : song

① movie ② hear ③ future
④ buy ⑤ brain

3 ________________ : fall = sport : football

① spring ② season ③ autumn
④ leaf ⑤ winter

4 hungry : ________________ = thick : thin

① food ② sleepy ③ family
④ dead ⑤ full

5 make : card = ________________ : hand

① foot ② wash ③ right
④ break ⑤ business

D 문맥에 맞게 다음 문장을 완성하세요.

1	Harry is planting •	• a	sports camp next week.
2	I'm sorry •	• b	for your time.
3	Thank you very much •	• c	but I can't go to the party.
4	My sister will join a winter •	• d	to LA next week.
5	I will go on a business trip •	• e	a tree in his garden.

E 문장을 읽고 문맥에 적절한 단어를 고르세요.

1 This bread tastes better with (a) (butter/card) on it.

2 I am very (hungry/sorry). I have to eat something.

3 I need my own (brand/camera) to take pictures of the spring flowers.

4 If you do not give water to the flowers, they will soon be (dead/full).

5 This book is (thin/sorry) but it will take time to understand.

F 문장의 빈칸에 알맞은 단어를 〈보기〉에서 찾아 쓰세요. (필요하면 형태를 고치세요.)

보기 ticket art visit grandparents nurse

1 Last Saturday, our class ____________ a history museum.
지난 토요일에 우리 반은 역사 박물관을 방문했다.

2 My dad gave me two free movie ____________.
아빠가 나에게 두 장의 무료 영화표를 주셨다.

3 The ____________ was kind to all the people in the hospital.
그 간호사는 병원에 있는 모든 사람에게 친절했다.

4 Yesterday, my ______________ and I went on a picnic to a park.
어제 조부모님과 나는 공원으로 소풍을 갔다.

5 My dream is to put my paintings in famous ____________ galleries.
내 꿈은 내 그림을 유명한 미술관에 전시하는 하는 것이다.

G 그림에 해당하는 낱말을 〈보기〉에서 골라 쓰세요.

1 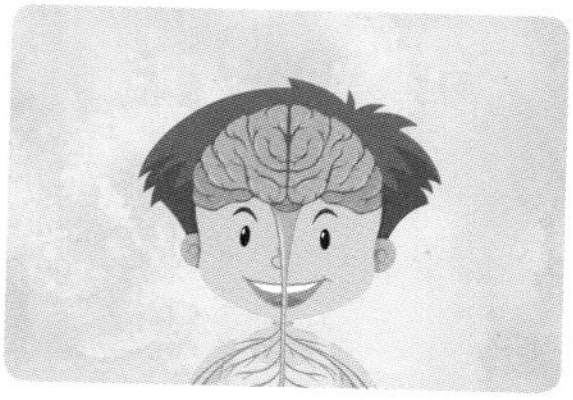

(   )

2 

(   )

3 

(   )

4 

(   )

5 

(   )

6 

(   )

보기 bridge write thick brain dead family

Study More

명사와 동사의 형태가 같은 단어들

- [break] 명 휴식 동 ~을 부수다/깨다/고장내다
  take a **break** 휴식을 취하다 **break** a plate 접시를 깨다
- [plant] 명 식물 동 ~을 심다
  a desert **plant** 사막 식물 **plant** roses in a garden 정원에 장미를 심다

Day 11

MP3

201 **plane** [plein]

명 비행기

travel by plane 비행기로 여행하다
the plane for Seoul 서울행 비행기

202 **slow** [slou]

형 느린 slow-slower-slowest 부 slowly 느리게

a slow beat 느린 박자 walk slowly 천천히 걷다

203 **strong** [strɔ(:)ŋ]

형 강한 strong-stronger-strongest

a strong country 강한 나라 a strong man 힘이 센 사람

204 **weak** [wi:k]

형 약한 weak-weaker-weakest

a weak heart 약한 심장 a weak table 약한 탁자

205 **go** [gou]

동 가다 go-went-gone

go to school 학교에 가다 go for a walk 산책 하다

206 **pilot** [páilət]

명 조종사

become a pilot 조종사가 되다 an airline pilot 항공사 조종사

207 **chance** [tʃæns]

명 기회

another chance 다른 기회 give a chance 기회를 주다

208 **bake** [beik]

동 굽다 bake-baked-baked

bake bread 빵을 굽다 bake potatoes 감자를 굽다

209 **congratulate** [kəngrǽtʃəlèit]

동 축하하다 congratulate-congratulated-congratulated

congratulate a new king 새 왕을 축하하다
congratulate you on your birthday 당신의 생일을 축하하다

210 **fast** [fæst]

형 빠른 부 빠르게, 빨리 fast-faster-fastest

walk fast 빠르게 걷다 run fast 빠르게 뛰다

Daily Test

| 월 일 |

A 우리말에 맞게 빈 칸에 알맞은 단어를 쓰세요.

1 Dad left for Jeju Island by ________________. 아빠는 비행기로 제주도에 가셨다.

2 John is walking ________________. John은 느리게 걷는 중이다.

3 My friend Ted is as ________________ as his father.
내 친구 Ted는 그의 아빠만큼 힘이 세다.

4 This ladder is too ________________ to climb up. 이 사다리는 올라가기에는 너무 약하다.

5 Let's ________________ to the beach. 해변으로 갑시다.

6 Minhyuk became a ________________. 민혁이는 조종사가 되었다.

7 I'll give him one more ________________. 나는 그에게 한 번의 기회를 더 줄 것이다.

8 Billy ________________ a chocolate cake for his family.
Billy는 그의 가족을 위해 초콜릿 케이크를 구웠다.

9 I ________________ you on your birthday, Jim! Jim, 생일을 축하해!

10 Tim can run ________________ than Jihoon. Tim은 지훈보다 빠르게 뛸 수 있다.

B 빈 칸에 알맞은 단어를 고르세요.

1 The red table has ________________ legs.
① cold ② weak ③ bake ④ warm ⑤ check

2 We ________________ our team on their victory.
① congratulated ② went ③ cared ④ stopped ⑤ stretched

3 I'm ________________ a cake for my son.
① congratulate ② baking ③ checking ④ breathing ⑤ center

Day 11

MP3

211 **warm** [wɔːrm]

형 따뜻한 warm-warmer-warmest

warm weather 따뜻한 날씨 a warm coat 따뜻한 코트

212 **stretch** [stretʃ]

동 뻗다 stretch-stretched-stretched

stretch your leg 다리를 뻗다
stretch the right hand 오른손을 뻗다

213 **bye** [bai]

감 안녕

say good-bye 작별 인사 하다 Bye for now, Kelly! 나중에 봐, Kelly!

214 **care** [kɛər]

동 돌보다 명 돌봄, 보살핌 care-cared-cared

care for children 아이들을 돌보다 Take care! 잘 지내!

215 **center** [séntər]

명 중심, 중앙

the center of the table 탁자의 중앙
the center of a circle 원의 중심

216 **bring** [briŋ]

동 가져오다 bring-brought-brought

bring books 책을 가져오다
bring the present for Yuri 유리를 위한 선물을 가져오다

217 **church** [tʃəːrtʃ]

명 교회

go to church 교회에 가다 a church tower 교회 탑

218 **check** [tʃek]

동 확인하다 check-checked-checked

check your answer 정답을 확인하다
check the lunch menu 점심 메뉴를 확인하다

219 **stop** [stɑp]

동 멈추다 stop-stopped-stopped

stop a car 차를 멈추다 stop a fight 싸움을 멈추다

220 **cartoon** [kɑːrtúːn]

명 만화

children's cartoons 어린이 만화영화
an educational cartoon 교육용 만화

Daily Test

| 월 일 |

A 우리말에 맞게 빈 칸에 알맞은 단어를 쓰세요.

1 It's a ______________ and sunny day. 오늘은 따뜻하고 맑은 날이다.

2 ______________ out your arms like this. 이렇게 팔을 뻗어 보세요.

3 ______________, Helen. See you next week. 안녕, Helen, 다음주에 보자.

4 Amy ______________ for her sister yesterday. Amy는 어제 그녀의 여동생을 돌봤다.

5 There is a tall tree in the ______________ of the park.
공원 중앙에는 큰 나무 한 그루가 있다.

6 ______________ him some oranges. 그에게 오렌지를 좀 가져다 주세요.

7 Mina goes to ______________ on Sundays. 미나는 일요일마다 교회에 간다.

8 Did you ______________ the time table? 시간표 확인했습니까?

9 The policeman ______________ the truck. 경찰관이 그 트럭을 멈추어 세웠다.

10 The ______________ is famous among children.
그 만화영화는 아이들 사이에서 유명하다.

B 빈 칸에 알맞은 단어를 고르세요.

1 Don't forget to ______________ your coat.
① bring ② slow ③ strong ④ fast ⑤ purple

2 It ______________ snowing.
① stretched ② brought ③ stopped ④ carried ⑤ went

3 Mickey Mouse is a popular Disney ______________.
① church ② chance ③ stretch ④ cartoon ⑤ weak

Day 12

MP3

221 **date** [deit]

명 날짜, 데이트

date and time 날짜와 시간 change the date 날짜를 바꾸다

222 **drive** [draiv]

동 운전하다 drive-drove-driven

drive a taxi 택시를 운전하다 drive a car 자동차를 운전하다

223 **brave** [breiv]

형 용감한 brave-braver-bravest

a brave man 용감한 사람 a brave soldier 용감한 군인

224 **brown** [braun]

형 갈색의 명 갈색

brown hair 갈색 머리 light brown 연한 갈색

225 **aunt** [ænt]

명 이모, 숙모, 고모

my aunt's house 우리 고모의 집
talk with her aunt 그녀의 이모와 얘기를 나누다

226 **butterfly** [bʌ́tərflài]

명 나비

catch a butterfly 나비를 잡다
a butterfly on the flower 꽃 위의 나비

227 **chew** [tʃuː]

동 씹다 chew-chewed-chewed

chew food 음식을 씹다 chew gum 껌을 씹다

228 **introduce** [ìntrədjúːs]

동 소개하다 introduce-introduced-introduced

introduce my friend 내 친구를 소개하다
introduce a new book 새로운 책을 소개하다

229 **jump** [dʒʌmp]

동 뛰다 jump-jumped-jumped

jump up 뛰어오르다 jump high 높이 뛰다

230 **off** [ɔːf]

부 떨어져, (무엇이) 제거되어

take+명(의복)+off ~을 벗다 take your hat off 모자를 벗다

Daily Test

| 월 일 |

A 우리말에 맞게 빈 칸에 알맞은 단어를 쓰세요.

1 What's the ________________ today? 오늘이 며칠인가요?

2 Can you ________________? 운전 할 줄 아시나요?

3 Firefighters are very ________________. 소방관들은 매우 용감하다.

4 We saw a ________________ bear at the zoo. 우리는 동물원에서 갈색 곰을 보았다.

5 My ________________ lives in Japan. 우리 고모는 일본에 살고 있다.

6 There is a ________________ on the flower. 꽃 위에 나비가 있다.

7 He is always ________________ gum. 그는 항상 껌을 씹고 있다.

8 Let me ________________ myself. 제 소개를 하겠습니다.

9 A frog can ________________ high. 개구리는 높게 뛸 수 있다.

10 Take your coat ________________. 코트를 벗어라.

B 빈 칸에 알맞은 단어를 고르세요.

1 Don't ________________ so fast.

① chewing ② enjoy ③ drive ④ brave ⑤ scary

2 Can you take your shoes ________________?

① high ② jump ③ with ④ off ⑤ chew

3 I'll ________________ my sister to you.

① introduce ② curly ③ brave ④ aunt ⑤ surf

Day 12

MP3

231 **homework** [hóumwə̀ːrk]

명 숙제

history homework 역사 숙제
do your homework 숙제를 하다

232 **surf** [səːrf]

동 파도타기를 하다, 인터넷을 검색하다 surf-surfed-surfed

go surfing 파도타기를 하러 가다
surf the Internet 인터넷을 검색하다

233 **enjoy** [indʒɔ́i]

동 즐기다 enjoy-enjoyed-enjoyed

enjoy movies 영화를 즐기다
enjoy the winter vacation 겨울방학을 즐기다

234 **party** [páːrti]

명 파티

a farewell party 송별파티
Jim's birthday party Jim의 생일 파티

235 **corner** [kɔ́ːrnər]

명 모퉁이

at a street corner 거리의 모퉁이에
around the corner 길 모퉁이를 돈 곳에

236 **curly** [kə́ːrli]

형 구불구불한 curly-curlier-curliest

long curly hair 긴 곱슬 머리 a curly tail 구불구불한 꼬리

237 **curtain** [kə́ːrtən]

명 커튼

close the curtains 커튼을 치다 hang curtains 커튼을 달다

238 **bright** [brait]

형 밝은, 똑똑한 bright-brighter-brightest

a bright star 밝은 별 a bright student 똑똑한 학생

239 **deep** [diːp]

형 깊은 deep-deeper-deepest

a deep river 깊은 강 a deep valley 깊은 계곡

240 **scary** [skɛ́(ː)əri]

형 무서운 scary-scarier-scariest

a scary story 무서운 이야기 look scary 무섭게 보인다

Daily Test

| 월 일 |

A 우리말에 맞게 빈 칸에 알맞은 단어를 쓰세요.

1 Students are doing their ________________. 학생들은 그들의 숙제를 하는 중이다.

2 They ________________ the Internet. 그들은 인터넷을 검색했다.

3 I ________________ taking a walk with my dog. 나는 강아지와 산책을 즐겼다.

4 Jim had a birthday ________________ last week. Jim은 지난 주에 생일 파티를 했다.

5 Turn left at the first ________________. 첫 번째 모퉁이에서 좌회전 하세요.

6 Amy has short brown ________________ hair. Amy는 짧은 갈색 곱슬머리이다.

7 Mom hung ________________ in my room. 엄마는 내 방에 커튼을 달았다.

8 Harry is a ________________ student in class. Harry는 교실에서 똑똑한 학생이다.

9 Don't go in the ________________ water. 깊은 물가로 가지 마라.

10 I don't like to watch ________________ movies. 나는 무서운 영화를 보는 것을 싫어한다.

B 빈 칸에 알맞은 단어를 고르세요.

1 The stars were very ________________ last night.
① thick ② bright ③ scary ④ deep ⑤ thin

2 Kate ________________ playing soccer.
① introduces ② surfs ③ drives ④ enjoys ⑤ jumps

3 The pool is too ________________ to swim in.
① bright ② thin ③ full ④ brave ⑤ deep

Review Test 06

A **우리말에 맞게 빈 칸에 알맞은 단어를 쓰세요.**

1 a ________________ heart 약한 심장

2 another ________________ 다른 기회

3 ________________ you on your birthday 당신의 생일을 축하하다

4 the ________________ of a circle 원의 중심

5 ________________ the lunch menu 점심 메뉴를 확인하다

6 a ________________ star 밝은 별

7 ________________ gum 껌을 씹다

8 ________________ the winter vacation 겨울방학을 즐기다

9 change the ________________ 날짜를 바꾸다

10 a ________________ river 깊은 강

B **다음 영어 풀이에 알맞은 어휘를 〈보기〉에서 고르세요.**

보기	party	pilot	aunt	stretch	bake

1 ____________ : to make something longer or wider

2 ____________ : a person who flies an airplane or helicopter

3 ____________ : to cook food such as cake or bread in an oven

4 ____________ : the sister of your father or mother, or the wife of your uncle

5 ____________ : a gathering of people to have fun and pleasure

C 다음 단어의 관계가 A:B=C:D가 되도록 알맞은 단어를 골라 빈 칸에 적으세요.

1 brave : soldier = ______________ : story

① scary ② introduce ③ chance
④ care ⑤ bring

2 chew : gum = ______________ : myself

① I ② weak ③ introduce
④ mine ⑤ say

3 bring : ______________ = bake : baked

① brought ② bought ③ bringed
④ broughted ⑤ bringing

4 ______________ : Internet = enjoy : party

① go ② slow ③ take
④ curly ⑤ surf

5 yellow : brown = ant : ______________

① black ② animal ③ dog
④ butterfly ⑤ small

D 문맥에 맞게 다음 문장을 완성하세요.

1	Dad left for Jeju Island •	• a	by plane.
2	Billy baked a chocolate •	• b	your arms like this.
3	Stretch out •	• c	brown curly hair.
4	A frog can •	• d	cake for his family.
5	Amy has short •	• e	jump high.

E 문장을 읽고 문맥에 적절한 단어를 고르세요.

1 Lucy is (caring/surfing) for a little cat.

2 My father (goes/surfs) to work by car.

3 The old woman (stopped/jumped) a boy to ask for help.

4 Brian, I have to sleep now. Can you (enjoy/close) the curtain for me?

5 We will have a farewell (bye/party) because Tim is moving to another school.

F 문장의 빈칸에 알맞은 단어를 〈보기〉에서 찾아 쓰세요. (필요하면 형태를 고치세요.)

보기	brown	corner	warm	scary	strong

1 The water is now ____________ enough to take a bath.
이제 목욕하기에 적당할 정도로 물이 따뜻하다.

2 I could not open my umbrella because the wind was very ____________.
바람이 아주 강해서 우산을 펼 수가 없었다.

3 A black dog was running around the ____________.
검은 개 한 마리가 모퉁이를 돌아 뛰고 있었다.

4 My mother bought me a ____________ sweater for my birthday.
어머니는 내 생일날 내게 갈색 스웨터를 사 주셨다.

5 Last night, Jiyong read a very ____________ story to us.
지난 밤에 지용은 우리에게 아주 무서운 이야기를 읽어 주었다.

G 그림과 낱말이 잘못 짝지어진 것을 고르세요. ……………………………………………… (　　　　)

ⓐ

church

ⓑ

fast

ⓒ

pilot

ⓓ

drive

H 낱말과 어울리는 그림을 연결하세요.

1 drive •

2 jump •

• ⓐ

• ⓑ

Study More

stop의 용법

- [stop+동명사] : '~하는 것을 멈추다'
  I **stopped eating** late at night. 나는 밤 늦게 먹는 것을 그만 두었다.
- [stop to+동사] : '~하기 위해 멈추다'
  I **stopped to eat** lunch at the restaurant. 나는 그 식당에서 점심을 먹기 위해 멈추었다.

Day 13

MP3

241 **country** [kʌ́ntri]

명 나라, 시골

in the country 시골에서　the Asian countries 아시아 국가들

242 **doll** [dɑl]

명 인형

a paper doll 종이 인형　play dolls 인형놀이 하다

243 **busy** [bízi]

형 바쁜　busy - busier - busiest

a busy day 바쁜 날　a busy schedule 바쁜 일정

244 **free** [friː]

형 자유로운

be free 자유롭다　set free 자유롭게 해주다

245 **early** [ə́ːrli]

형 이른　부 일찍　early - earlier - earliest

early spring 이른 봄　get up early 일찍 일어나다

246 **late** [leit]

형 늦은　부 늦게　late - later - latest

in the late afternoon 늦은 오후　late at night 밤 늦게, 밤 늦도록

247 **round** [raund]

형 둥근　round - rounder - roundest

a round table 둥근 탁자　a round hat 둥근 모자

248 **live** [liv]

동 살다　live - lived - lived

live in ~에 살다　live a happy life 행복한 삶을 살다

249 **back** [bæk]

명 뒤　부 다시 돌아와서

the back of a car 차의 뒷부분　come back 돌아오다

250 **ball** [bɔːl]

명 공

catch a ball 공을 잡다　a ball game 공놀이

Daily Test

| 월 일 |

A 우리말에 맞게 빈 칸에 알맞은 단어를 쓰세요.

1 Which ______________ do you want to go to? 어떤 나라에 가고 싶나요?

2 Some girls are playing with ______________. 몇몇 소녀들은 인형놀이를 하는 중이다.

3 Are you ______________ today? 오늘 바쁘신가요?

4 Are you ______________ tonight? 오늘 밤에 시간 있니?

5 Minji's birthday is in ______________ April. 민지의 생일은 4월 초다.

6 Don't go out alone ______________ at night. 늦은 밤에 혼자 나가지 말아라.

7 The ______________ hat is mine. 저 둥근 모자는 내 것이다.

8 Peter ______________ in Seoul. Peter는 서울에 산다.

9 Amy will come ______________ home tomorrow. Amy는 내일 집에 돌아올 것이다.

10 The little boy threw the ______________ over the fence.
어린 소년이 담장 밖으로 공을 던졌다.

B 빈 칸에 알맞은 단어를 고르세요.

1 Jane set the bird ______________.
① free ② noon ③ whole ④ late ⑤ early

2 When did you come ______________ home?
① late ② wish ③ back ④ country ⑤ ready

3 I'm so ______________ today.
① busy ② back ③ hate ④ whole ⑤ together

Day 13

MP3

251 **circle** [sə́:rkl]

명 원

draw a circle 원을 그리다 stand in a circle 둥글게 서다

252 **ready** [rédi]

형 준비가 된

be ready to+동사원형 ~할 준비가 되다

be ready to go on a picnic 소풍 갈 준비가 되다

253 **newspaper** [njú:zpèipər]

명 신문

a weekly newspaper 주간 신문

today's newspaper 오늘의 신문

254 **read** [ri:d]

동 읽다 read-read-read

read a poem aloud 시를 크게 읽다

read an interesting story 재미있는 이야기를 읽다

255 **whole** [houl]

형 전체의

the whole day 종일 the whole country 전국

256 **noon** [nu:n]

명 낮 12시, 정오

at noon 정오에 before noon 오전에

257 **wish** [wiʃ]

명 소원 동 바라다, 원하다 wish-wished-wished

make a wish 소원을 빌다 Jane's wish Jane의 소원

258 **world** [wə:rld]

명 세계

all over the world 전 세계에서

travel around the world 세계일주를 하다

259 **worry** [wə́:ri]

동 걱정하다 명 걱정, 근심 worry-worried-worried

Don't worry. 걱정하지 마세요. a serious worry 심각한 걱정

260 **together** [təgéðər]

부 함께, 같이

happy together 함께 행복한 study together 함께 공부하다

Daily Test

| 월 일 |

A 우리말에 맞게 빈 칸에 알맞은 단어를 쓰세요.

1 The boy is drawing a ______________. 소년은 원을 그리는 중이다.

2 Are you ______________ to start studying for the exam? 시험 공부를 시작 할 준비가 되었니?

3 I read about the food in a ______________. 나는 신문에서 그 음식에 대해 읽었다.

4 Sam likes to ______________ books to his daughter. Sam은 딸에게 책 읽어주는 것을 좋아한다.

5 He spent the ______________ day repairing his bike. 그는 종일 그의 자전거를 고쳤다.

6 We will meet at ______________. 우리는 낮 12시에 만날 것이다.

7 I ______________ you good luck. 너의 행운을 빌게.

8 I have a dream to travel all over the ______________. 나는 전 세계를 여행하는 꿈이 있다.

9 I ______________ about the science test. 나는 과학 시험이 걱정된다.

10 Let's study ______________! 함께 공부하자!

B 빈 칸에 알맞은 단어를 고르세요.

1 Matthew and I grew ______________.

① round ② ball ③ live ④ circle ⑤ together

2 Are you ______________ to go?

① circle ② worry ③ ready ④ early ⑤ country

3 Don't ______________, be happy.

① round ② back ③ noon ④ worry ⑤ enjoy

Day 14

MP3

261 **poor** [puər]

형 가난한, 불쌍한 poor-poorer-poorest

poor people 가난한 사람들 a poor kitten 불쌍한 새끼고양이

262 **sweet** [swiːt]

형 달콤한 sweet-sweeter-sweetest

sweet tea 달콤한 차 sweet candy 달콤한 사탕

263 **laugh** [læf]

명 웃음 동 웃다 laugh-laughed-laughed

give a laugh 웃다 make me laugh 나를 웃게 만들다

264 **duck** [dʌk]

명 오리

a wild duck 야생 오리 a duck egg 거위 알

265 **candy** [kǽndi]

명 사탕

cotton candy 솜사탕 a box of candy 사탕 한 상자

266 **spicy** [spáisi]

형 매운

spicy food 매운 음식 spicy sauce 매운 소스

267 **look** [luk]

동 보다 look-looked-looked

look at a fish 물고기를 보다
look out the window 창 밖을 보다

268 **fan** [fæn]

명 팬, 선풍기

movie fans 영화 팬 an electric fan 선풍기

269 **upset** [ʌpsét]

형 속상한

be very upset 매우 속상하다 feel upset 화가 나다

270 **win** [win]

동 이기다 win-won-won

win a game 게임에서 이기다 win a contest 경기에서 이기다

Daily Test

| 월 일 |

A 우리말에 맞게 빈 칸에 알맞은 단어를 쓰세요.

1 We should help ________________ people. 우리는 가난한 사람들을 도와야 한다.

2 This cake tastes ________________. 이 케이크는 달콤하다.

3 Amy started to ________________ loudly. Amy는 크게 웃기 시작했다.

4 ________________ like to live near water. 오리는 물가에서 사는 것을 좋아한다.

5 The English teacher gave us some ________________ and chocolates. 영어 선생님은 우리에게 약간의 사탕과 초콜릿들을 주셨다.

6 This sauce is too ________________. 이 소스는 너무 맵다.

7 Minsu ________________ up at the blue sky. 민수는 푸른 하늘을 바라보았다.

8 I use an electric ________________ to cool the room. 나는 방을 시원하게 하기 위해서 선풍기를 사용한다.

9 James was very ________________ about his math exam result. James는 수학시험 결과에 매우 화가 났다.

10 We ________________ the soccer game! 우리는 축구 경기에서 이겼어!

B 빈 칸에 알맞은 단어를 고르세요.

1 Kim's family was very ________________.

① laugh ② win ③ poor ④ drop ⑤ behind

2 We will ________________ the baseball game next month.

① look ② win ③ behind ④ won ⑤ poor

3 There is a cup of ________________ cocoa milk on the table.

① upset ② wish ③ excuse ④ sweet ⑤ candy

Day 14

MP3

271 **pay** [pei]

동 지불하다 pay-paid-paid

pay for food 음식값을 지불하다
pay for tickets 표 값을 지불하다

272 **child** [tʃaild]

명 아이 복 children

a child reporter 어린이 기자 many children 많은 아이들

273 **tooth** [tu:θ]

명 이, 치아 복 teeth

a toothbrush 칫솔 brush your teeth 이를 닦다

274 **drop** [drɑp]

명 방울 동 떨어뜨리다 drop-dropped-dropped

a drop of water 물 한 방울 drop a cup 컵을 떨어뜨리다

275 **factory** [fǽktəri]

명 공장

a car factory 자동차 공장 build a factory 공장을 짓다

276 **rich** [ritʃ]

형 부유한 rich-richer-richest

a rich man 부자 a rich country 부유한 나라

277 **excuse** [ikskjú:s]

명 변명 동 변명하다, 용서하다 excuse-excused-excused

make an excuse 변명하다 excuse me 실례합니다

278 **errand** [érənd]

명 심부름

go on an errand / run an errand 심부름을 하다

279 **famous** [féiməs]

형 유명한 famous-more famous-most famous

a famous movie star 유명한 영화 배우
a famous soccer player 유명한 축구 선수

280 **behind** [biháind]

전 뒤에 부 뒤로, 뒤에

behind the hospital 병원 뒤에 look behind 뒤를 보시오

Daily Test

| 월 일 |

A 우리말에 맞게 빈 칸에 알맞은 단어를 쓰세요.

1 I'll ______________ for the tickets. 내가 표 값을 지불할게요.

2 Who is the ______________ on the left? 왼쪽에 있는 아이는 누구니?

3 Fiona has a loose ______________. Fiona는 이가 흔들린다.

4 Ann ______________ her cup. Ann은 컵을 떨어뜨렸다.

5 He works at a watch ______________. 그는 시계 공장에서 일한다.

6 Harry looks very ______________. Harry는 매우 부자인 것처럼 보인다.

7 ______________ me. Where is the nearest subway station?
실례합니다. 가장 가까운 지하철 역이 어디에 있나요?

8 I'm going on an ______________. 나는 심부름을 하는 중이다.

9 Ji-sung Park is a ______________ soccer player. 박지성은 유명한 축구 선수이다.

10 The post office is ______________ the bank. 우체국은 은행 뒤에 있다.

B 빈 칸에 알맞은 단어를 고르세요.

1 He is a ______________ baseball player in Korea.
① drop ② laugh ③ famous ④ tooth ⑤ errand

2 He ______________ 10,000 won for the pants.
① paid ② dropped ③ laughed ④ excused ⑤ went

3 ______________ me. Where is the post office?
① Excuse ② Drop ③ Hello ④ Behind ⑤ Know

Review Test 07

Day 13 + Day 14 | 월 일 |

A 우리말에 맞게 빈 칸에 알맞은 단어를 쓰세요.

1 a ________________ schedule 바쁜 일정

2 in the ________________ afternoon 늦은 오후

3 ________________ a poem aloud 시를 크게 읽다

4 the ________________ country 전국

5 before ________________ 오전에

6 ________________ people 가난한 사람들

7 make me ________________ 나를 웃게 만들다

8 feel ________________ 화가 나다

9 make an ________________ 변명하다

10 ________________ the hospital 병원 뒤에

B 다음 영어 풀이에 알맞은 어휘를 〈보기〉에서 고르세요.

보기	doll	fan	country	child	newspaper

1 ____________ : an area where people live under the same government

2 ____________ : a kind of toy that looks like a baby or a person

3 ____________ : a paper which has news, information, and advertisements

4 ____________ : a device that makes wind by moving air with plastic hands

5 ____________ : a young boy or girl

C 다음 단어의 관계가 A:B=C:D가 되도록 알맞은 단어를 골라 빈 칸에 적으세요.

1 ________________ : Korea = toy : doll

① country ② ready ③ Seoul
④ whole ⑤ Japan

2 busy : ________________ = late : early

① worry ② laugh ③ drop
④ free ⑤ famous

3 ________________ : people = beautiful : dress

① open ② earth ③ rich
④ city ⑤ world

4 win : won = pay : ________________

① payed ② payied ③ pays
④ paily ⑤ paid

5 child : children = ________________ : teeth

① teeths ② tooth ③ toothes
④ teethes ⑤ toothed

D 문맥에 맞게 다음 문장을 완성하세요.

1	I use an electric •	• a	all over the world.
2	Are you ready •	• b	to start studying for the exam?
3	I have a dream to travel •	• c	a watch factory.
4	The little boy threw •	• d	fan to cool the room.
5	He works at •	• e	the ball over the fence.

E 문장을 읽고 문맥에 적절한 단어를 고르세요.

1 He (lives/reads) far away from his parents.

2 Many people gathered to move the fallen tree (late/together).

3 (Ducks/Dolls) and swans belong to the same bird family.

4 The little boy is (dropping/excusing) his mother's coins for fun.

5 The soccer player was (famous/spicy) for his unique kicking styles.

F 문장의 빈칸에 알맞은 단어를 〈보기〉에서 찾아 쓰세요. (필요하면 형태를 고치세요.)

보기 circle early errand round spicy

1 You should get up ____________ in the morning.
너는 아침에 일찍 일어나야 한다.

2 You don't have to draw a perfect ____________.
너는 완전한 원을 그릴 필요는 없어.

3 This pasta sauce is too ____________.
이 파스타 소스는 너무 맵다.

4 Don't forget that you have an ____________ to do!
심부름 할 것이 있다는 것 잊지 마!

5 I think that our new kitchen table should be a ____________ one.
새로운 식탁은 둥근 것이어야 할 것 같아.

G 그림에 해당하는 낱말을 〈보기〉에서 골라 쓰세요.

1 

(   )

2 

(   )

3 

(   )

4 

(   )

5 

(   )

6 

(   )

보기 | newspaper | look | worry | wish | win | back

Study More

음식의 맛이나 느낌에 대한 단어들

- flavors (맛) : salty 짠, bitter 쓴, spicy/hot 매운, sour 신, 시큼한
  salty water 짠 맛이 나는 물   **bitter** tablets 쓴맛이 나는 알약
- textures (질감) : creamy 크림 같은, crunchy 아삭(아삭)한, greasy 기름진, moist 촉촉한
  a **creamy** soup 크림 같은 수프   **crunchy** cookies 아삭아삭한 과자

Day 15

MP3

281 **red** [red]
형 붉은 명 빨강, 빨간색
a red rose 빨간 장미 a red car 빨간 자동차

282 **blood** [blʌd]
명 피
lose blood 피를 흘리다 blood pressure 혈압

283 **block** [blɑk]
명 큰 덩어리, 한 구획
a block of ice 얼음 한 덩어리
two blocks from here 이 곳으로부터 두 구획 떨어진 곳

284 **thing** [θiŋ]
명 물건
sweet things 달콤한 것들 many things 많은 것들

285 **monkey** [mʌ́ŋki]
명 원숭이
a little monkey 어린 원숭이
a monkey's long tail 원숭이의 긴 꼬리

286 **train** [trein]
명 기차
get on a train 기차를 타다 travel by train 기차로 여행하다

287 **contest** [kántest]
명 경연, 대회
a speech contest 말하기 대회 an art contest 미술 대회

288 **keep** [ki:p]
동 유지하다, 보유하다 keep-kept-kept
keep air fresh 공기를 신선하게 유지하다
keep an old ring 오래된 반지를 간직하다

289 **secret** [sí:krit]
명 비밀 형 비밀의
keep a secret 비밀을 지키다 top secret 일급 비밀의

290 **bad** [bæd]
형 나쁜 bad-worse-worst
bad news 나쁜 소식 bad habits 나쁜 습관

Daily Test

A 우리말에 맞게 빈 칸에 알맞은 단어를 쓰세요.

1 There are many ______________ roses in the garden.
정원에 많은 빨간 장미들이 있다.

2 ______________ is thicker than water. 피는 물보다 진하다.

3 Go straight two ______________ and turn right. 두 블록 직진해서 우회전 하세요.

4 Mary likes sweet ______________. Mary는 달콤한 것들을 좋아한다.

5 The ______________ are climbing the trees. 원숭이들이 나무를 오르고 있다.

6 I like to travel by ______________. 나는 기차로 여행하는 것을 좋아한다.

7 Jiyoung won first prize in the tennis ______________.
지영은 테니스 대회에서 일등을 했다.

8 Sally ______________ her bags in the closet. Sally는 자신의 가방을 옷장에 보관한다.

9 Can you keep a ______________? 비밀을 지킬 수 있습니까?

10 I have some ______________ news. 나쁜 소식이 있습니다.

B 빈 칸에 알맞은 단어를 고르세요.

1 Minji won the Best Singer's Award in the singing ______________.
① factory ② blood ③ contest ④ theater ⑤ secret

2 Mom ______________ old letters in the box.
① kept ② then ③ secret ④ block ⑤ throat

3 Jane tried to keep it ______________ from her husband.
① blocks ② secret ③ things ④ bloods ⑤ keep

Day 15

MP3

291 **near** [niər]

전 ~근처에 부 가까이 near-nearer-nearest

near the town 마을 근처에 come near 가까이 오다

292 **earth** [əːrθ]

명 지구

life on earth 지구의 생물 earth science 지구 과학

293 **tradition** [trədíʃən]

명 전통

Korean tradition 한국 전통 an old tradition 오래된 전통

294 **yet** [jet]

부 아직

Don't go yet. 아직 가지 마세요.
A: Are you ready? B: Not yet. 준비됐니? / 아직 안됐어.

295 **textbook** [tékstbùk]

명 교과서

a science textbook 과학 교과서
an English textbook 영어 교과서

296 **theater** [θí(ː)ətər]

명 극장

a movie theater 극장 go to the theater 극장에 가다

297 **then** [ðen]

부 그때

just then 바로 그때 since then 그때부터

298 **piece** [piːs]

명 조각

a piece of bread 빵 한 조각
three pieces of cheese 세 조각의 치즈

299 **throat** [θrout]

명 목구멍

have a sore throat 목감기에 걸리다
look at your throat 목구멍을 살펴보다

300 **tomorrow** [təmɔ́ːrou]

명 내일

See you tomorrow. 내일 보자.
tomorrow morning 내일 아침

Daily Test

| 월 일 |

A 우리말에 맞게 빈 칸에 알맞은 단어를 쓰세요.

1 Mike stands ________________ the tree. Mike는 나무 근처에 서 있다.

2 Let's save our ________________. 우리의 지구를 살리자.

3 Eating songpyon for Chuseok is a Korean ________________.
추석에 송편을 먹는 것은 한국의 전통이다.

4 I don't know anything ________________. 나는 아직 아무것도 모르겠다.

5 I lost my English ________________ yesterday. 나는 어제 영어 교과서를 잃어버렸다.

6 Charlie went to the ________________ with his mother.
Charlie는 그의 엄마와 함께 극장에 갔다.

7 See you ________________. 그때 보자.

8 She ordered two ________________ of cake with milk.
그녀는 케이크 두 조각과 우유를 주문했다.

9 I have a sore ________________. 나는 목감기에 걸렸다.

10 How about ________________ afternoon? 내일 오후는 어때요?

B 빈 칸에 알맞은 단어를 고르세요.

1 I will go fishing ________________.
① yet ② block ③ yesterday ④ tomorrow ⑤ then

2 Mike has not come ________________.
① far ② just ③ drop ④ yet ⑤ thing

3 Where is the ________________ subway station?
① nearest ② fastest ③ errand ④ yet ⑤ then

Day 16

MP3

301 **work** [wəːrk]
동 일하다 명 일, 작업 work-worked-worked
work hard 열심히 일하다 go to work 출근하다

302 **rest** [rest]
명 휴식 동 쉬다 rest-rested-rested
rest after work 일한 후에 쉬다
take a rest / have a rest 휴식 하다

303 **park** [pɑːrk]
명 공원
go to a park 공원에 가다 a park bench 공원 벤치

304 **swim** [swim]
명 수영 동 수영하다 swim-swam-swum
a swimming pool 수영장 swim in the sea 바다에서 수영하다

305 **beach** [biːtʃ]
명 해변
on the beach 해변가에서
walk along the beach 해변가를 걷다

306 **oven** [ʌ́vən]
명 오븐
in the oven 오븐 속에 an electric oven 전기 오븐

307 **restaurant** [réstərənt]
명 식당
go to a restaurant 식당에 가다
an Italian restaurant 이탈리아 식당

308 **president** [prézidənt]
명 대통령, 회장
a class president 학급 반장
the American President 미국 대통령

309 **student** [stjúːdənt]
명 학생
a clever student 영리한 학생
a high school student 고등학생

310 **design** [dizáin]
명 디자인 동 디자인하다 design-designed-designed
a new design 새로운 디자인 design a dress 드레스를 디자인하다

Daily Test

| 월 일 |

A 우리말에 맞게 빈 칸에 알맞은 단어를 쓰세요.

1 She has a lot of ________________ to do. 그녀는 할 일이 많이 있다.

2 Alex wanted to take a ________________. Alex는 쉬고 싶었다.

3 We went for a walk in the ________________. 우리는 공원에 산책하러 갔다.

4 Cathy goes ________________ twice a week. Cathy는 일주일에 두 번 수영을 간다.

5 Several students are walking on a ________________.
몇몇 학생들은 해변가를 걷는 중이다.

6 Put the pie in the ________________. 파이를 오븐 안에 넣어라.

7 We are going to go to the new Chinese ________________ tomorrow.
우리는 내일 새로 생긴 중국요리 식당에 갈 예정이다.

8 Yuna became our class ________________. 유나는 학급 반장이 되었다.

9 We have a new ________________ from Japan. 일본에서 온 새로운 학생이 있습니다.

10 Mom ________________ this dress for me. 엄마는 나를 위해 드레스를 디자인했다.

B 빈 칸에 알맞은 단어를 고르세요.

1 I go to ________________ by bus.
① secret ② oven ③ work ④ president ⑤ swim

2 Who ________________ the bridge?
① awoke ② swam ③ kept ④ designed ⑤ lived

3 They spent a day at the ________________.
① president ② round ③ beach ④ oven ⑤ swim

Day 16

MP3

311 **moon** [mu:n]

명 달

a full moon 보름달　moon light 달빛

312 **office** [ɔ́(:)fis]

명 사무실

a ticket office 매표소　in the office 사무실에서

313 **often** [ɔ́(:)fən]

부 종종, 자주

as often as possible 가능한 자주
often go to a park 종종 공원을 가다

314 **pool** [pu:l]

명 물 웅덩이

a swimming pool 수영장　a pool of water 물 웅덩이

315 **only** [óunli]

형 유일한　부 단지

an only daughter 외동딸　only for a day 단지 하루 동안

316 **orange** [ɔ́(:)rindʒ]

명 오렌지

orange juice 오렌지 주스　orange peel 오렌지 껍질

317 **meal** [mi:l]

명 식사

have a meal 식사를 하다　mealtime 식사시간

318 **seat** [si:t]

명 자리, 좌석

take a seat 자리에 앉다　an aisle seat 복도 좌석

319 **parade** [pəréid]

명 행진, 퍼레이드

have a parade 행진을 하다　a car parade 자동차 퍼레이드

320 **awake** [əwéik]

형 깨어있는　동 깨다　awake - awoke - awoken

stay awake 깨어 있다　awake at midnight 한밤중에 깨다

Daily Test

| 월 일 |

A 우리말에 맞게 빈 칸에 알맞은 단어를 쓰세요.

1 The full ______________ lit up the village. 보름달이 그 마을을 밝게 비추었다.

2 David is working in the ______________. David는 사무실에서 일하는 중이다.

3 She ______________ watches movies at home. 그녀는 종종 집에서 영화를 본다.

4 The boy jumped into the swimming ______________.
소년은 수영장으로 뛰어들었다.

5 They changed their classroom ______________ for a day.
그들은 단지 하루 동안만 교실을 바꿨다.

6 Would you like some ______________ juice? 오렌지 주스 좀 드실래요?

7 Enjoy your ______________. 식사를 즐기세요.

8 John sat back in his ______________. John은 그의 자리로 돌아와 앉았다.

9 Students are having a ______________ outside. 학생들은 밖에서 행진을 하는 중이다.

10 Sarah stayed ______________ all night. Sarah는 밤새 깨어 있었다.

B 빈 칸에 알맞은 단어를 고르세요.

1 I had a ______________ with my family.
① restaurant ② seat ③ meal ④ work ⑤ moon

2 We ______________ go camping in summer.
① seat ② often ③ parade ④ like ⑤ awake

3 This is the ______________ restaurant around here.
① together ② only ③ yet ④ train ⑤ never

A 우리말에 맞게 빈 칸에 알맞은 단어를 쓰세요.

1 a speech ________________ 말하기 대회

2 ________________ air fresh 공기를 신선하게 유지하다

3 Korean ________________ 한국의 전통

4 Don't go ________________ 아직 가지 마세요

5 just ________________ 바로 그때

6 ________________ hard 열심히 일하다

7 a new ________________ 새로운 디자인

8 ________________ for a day 단지 하루 동안

9 have a ________________ 식사를 하다

10 stay ________________ 깨어 있다

B 다음 영어 풀이에 알맞은 어휘를 〈보기〉에서 고르세요.

보기	contest	oven	park	throat	seat

1 ____________ : the tube inside your mouth through which food passes to the stomach

2 ____________ : an open place or land for people to take a walk and exercise

3 ____________ : a cooking device used for baking bread or roasting meat

4 ____________ : an object or a piece of furniture made for sitting on

5 ____________ : a race or game in which people try to win or to do better than others

C 다음 단어의 관계가 A:B=C:D가 되도록 알맞은 단어를 골라 빈 칸에 적으세요.

1 full : ______________ = white : snow

① black ② moon ③ ground
④ fruit ⑤ pen

2 block : ice = ______________ : pizza

① chocolate ② cake ③ milk
④ piece ⑤ two

3 win : contest = keep : ______________

① secret ② theater ③ yet
④ throat ⑤ pool

4 good : bad = ______________ : far

① only ② near ③ seat
④ then ⑤ awake

5 swim : ______________ = eat : restaurant

① tradition ② thing ③ forest
④ sun ⑤ beach

D 문맥에 맞게 다음 문장을 완성하세요.

1 Go straight two blocks •	• a	with his mother.
2 Charlie went to the theater •	• b	take a rest.
3 Alex wanted to •	• c	having a parade outside.
4 Yuna became •	• d	and turn right.
5 Students are •	• e	our class president.

E 문장을 읽고 문맥에 적절한 단어를 고르세요.

1 She began to cry after hearing the (near/bad) news.

2 He coughed a lot and got a sore (throat/orange).

3 It is dangerous to (swim/awake) alone in the sea.

4 We had dinner at a good Italian (restaurant/beach) on my mother's birthday.

5 She (yet/often) goes to the library to read new books.

F 문장의 빈칸에 알맞은 단어를 〈보기〉에서 찾아 쓰세요. (필요하면 형태를 고치세요.)

보기	monkey	pool	office	textbook	tomorrow

1 He came to my ____________ to talk with me.
그는 나와 이야기 하기 위해 내 사무실로 왔다.

2 Several ____________ were climbing the trees.
몇 마리의 원숭이가 나무에 오르고 있었다.

3 Reading ____________ carefully will help your study.
교과서를 주의 깊게 읽는 것은 여러분의 공부를 도와줄 것입니다.

4 It's too late today. Let us leave ____________ morning then.
오늘은 너무 늦었어. 내일 아침에 떠나자.

5 The boys jumped into the swimming ____________ one after another.
소년들은 한 사람씩 수영장으로 뛰어 들었다.

G 그림과 낱말이 잘못 짝지어진 것을 고르세요. .... (   )

ⓐ

blood

ⓑ

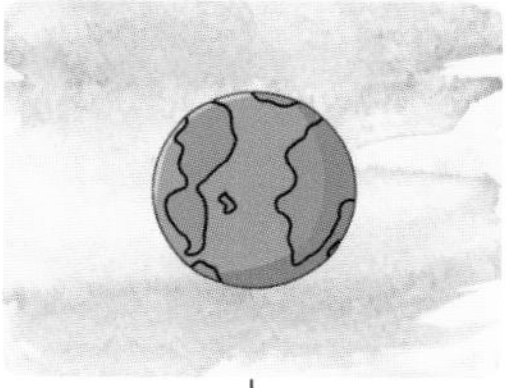

earth

ⓒ

theater

ⓓ

train

H 낱말과 어울리는 그림을 연결하세요.

1 swim •

2 orange •

• ⓐ

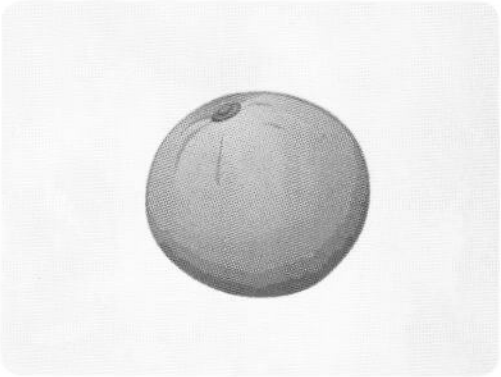

• ⓑ

Study More

secret의 다양한 쓰임

- [keep a secret] : '비밀을 지키다'   [keep something a secret] : '~을 비밀로 하다'
  Can you **keep it a secret**? 너는 그것을 비밀로 할 수 있니?
- [in secret] : '비밀리에, 비밀스럽게'
  They practiced the song **in secret.** 그들은 그 곡을 비밀리에 연습했다.

Day 17

MP3

321 **top** [tɑp]

명 꼭대기, 정상 반 bottom 바닥

at the top of the tower 탑의 꼭대기
at the top of the mountain 산 꼭대기

322 **see** [siː]

동 보다 see-saw-seen

See you again. 다음에 또 만나자. see a movie 영화를 보다

323 **blind** [blaind]

형 시각 장애의

a blind school 맹인 학교 a blind person 시각 장애인

324 **police** [pəlíːs]

명 경찰

a police officer 경찰관 a police car 경찰차

325 **fire** [fáiər]

명 불

a big fire 큰 불 make a fire 불을 내다

326 **paint** [peint]

동 색을 칠하다 paint-painted-painted

paint a picture 그림을 그리다
paint a table white 탁자를 흰 색으로 칠하다

327 **wall** [wɔːl]

명 벽

clean the wall 벽을 청소하다
a picture on the wall 벽 위의 그림

328 **rock** [rɑk]

명 바위

a big rock 큰 바위 a piece of rock 바위 한 조각

329 **stick** [stik]

명 막대기

a walking stick 지팡이 a hockey stick 하키용 스틱

330 **treat** [triːt]

명 대접 동 대하다, 대접하다 treat-treated-treated

a special treat 특별한 대우
treat animals with care 동물을 조심해서 다루다

Daily Test

| 월 일 |

A 우리말에 맞게 빈 칸에 알맞은 단어를 쓰세요.

1 The scene from the ______________ of the mountain was beautiful.
산 정상에서 보는 경치는 아름다웠다.

2 We'd like to ______________ the Eiffel Tower. 우리는 에펠 탑을 보고 싶다.

3 Guide dogs help ______________ people. 안내견은 시각장애인들을 돕는다.

4 He wants to become a ______________ officer. 그는 경찰관이 되고 싶어한다.

5 There was a big ______________ at night. 밤에 큰 불이 났었다.

6 Sam is ______________ the door. Sam은 문에 색을 칠하고 있다.

7 Mom hung a picture on the ______________. 엄마는 벽에 그림을 걸었다.

8 A mountain road was blocked by a big ______________.
그 산길은 큰 바위로 막혀있었다.

9 My grandfather bought a new walking ______________.
우리 할아버지는 새로운 지팡이를 사셨다.

10 John never ______________ me badly. John은 내게 절대로 심하게 대하지 않았다.

B 빈 칸에 알맞은 단어를 고르세요.

1 She is ______________ in her right eye.
① shoulder ② sick ③ blind ④ see ⑤ tower

2 Josh ______________ his dog well.
① treated ② ship ③ the lot ④ fire ⑤ excused

3 Junsu is ______________ the wall.
① blind ② painting ③ fire ④ saw ⑤ stick

Day 17

MP3

331 airport [ɛ́ərpɔ̀ːrt]

명 공항

an international airport 국제 공항   at the airport 공항에서

332 museum [mju(ː)zí(ː)əm]

명 박물관

a science museum 과학 박물관   an art museum 미술관

333 sick [sik]

형 아픈

a sick child 아픈 아이   look sick 안색이 좋지 않다

334 everything [évriθìŋ]

대 모든 것   유 all 반 nothing 아무것도

everything in my bag 내 가방 속 모든 것들

everything about friendship 우정에 대한 모든 것

335 tonight [tənáit]

명 오늘 밤 부 오늘 밤에

early tonight 오늘 밤 일찍   go out tonight 오늘 밤에 외출하다

336 touch [tʌtʃ]

동 만지다, 접촉하다 명 연락, 접촉 touch-touched-touched

keep in touch 계속 연락하다

Don't touch the dog. 그 개를 만지지 마세요.

337 towel [táuəl]

명 수건

a bath towel 목욕 수건   a clean towel 깨끗한 수건

338 tower [taʊə(r)]

명 탑

the Eiffel Tower 에펠 탑   a clock tower 시계탑

339 ship [ʃip]

명 배

get on a ship 배를 타다   by ship 배로

340 shoulder [ʃóuldər]

명 어깨

the right shoulder 오른쪽 어깨   on the shoulder 어깨 위에

Daily Test

| 월 일 |

A 우리말에 맞게 빈 칸에 알맞은 단어를 쓰세요.

1 What time did you arrive at the ________________? 공항에 몇 시에 도착했나요?

2 I went to the National Science ________________ last Saturday.
지난 토요일에 난 국립 과학 박물관에 다녀왔다.

3 I was ________________ last week. 나는 지난 주에 아팠다.

4 ________________ on the dining table looks delicious.
식탁 위에 있는 모든 것이 맛있어 보인다.

5 Will you go out with us ________________? 오늘 밤에 우리랑 놀러 갈래?

6 Don't ________________ the pot. It's too hot. 주전자를 만지지 마세요. 그건 너무 뜨거워요.

7 She wiped her hands with a ________________. 그녀는 수건으로 손을 닦았다.

8 There is a clock ________________ on the hill. 언덕 위에 시계탑이 있다

9 We can go there by ________________. 우리는 배로 그 곳에 갈 수 있다.

10 Dad put his hand on my ________________ and smiled.
아빠는 내 어깨에 손을 얹고 미소를 지었다.

B 빈 칸에 알맞은 단어를 고르세요.

1 Minji looked so ________________.
① sick ② see ③ near ④ health ⑤ touch

2 Cathy ________________ the cat and smiled.
① treat ② touched ③ run ④ laughed ⑤ drove

3 I will go to Jeju Island by ________________.
① museum ② airport ③ towel ④ shoulder ⑤ ship

Day 18

MP3

341 **heavy** [hévi]

형 무거운 heavy-heavier-heaviest

have heavy rain 호우가 내리다
the noise of heavy traffic 교통 체증의 소음

342 **closet** [klázit]

명 옷장

my bedroom closet 내 방 침실 옷장　in the closet 옷장 속

343 **snack** [snæk]

명 간식

a delicious snack 맛있는 간식　eat a snack 간식을 먹다

344 **window** [wíndou]

명 창문

open a window 창문을 열다
break a window 창문을 부수다

345 **ask** [æsk]

동 묻다, 부탁하다 ask-asked-asked

ask a question 질문하다　ask for a favor 부탁하다

346 **price** [prais]

명 가격, 값

a low price 낮은 가격　the price of oranges 오렌지 가격

347 **problem** [prábləm]

명 문제

a social problem 사회 문제　solve a problem 문제를 해결하다

348 **drink** [driŋk]

동 마시다 명 음료 drink-drank-drunk

drink water 물을 마시다　soft drinks 청량 음료

349 **once** [wʌns]

부 한 번, 한때

once upon a time 옛날 옛적에　once a month 한 달에 한 번

350 **peach** [piːtʃ]

명 복숭아

peach jam 복숭아 잼　a peach tree 복숭아 나무

Daily Test

| 월 일 |

A 우리말에 맞게 빈 칸에 알맞은 단어를 쓰세요.

1 The man is lifting up the ______________ barbell.
남자가 무거운 역기를 들어 올리고 있다.

2 I found the ring in my ______________. 나는 내 옷장 속에서 반지를 찾았다.

3 Banana pie is Tim's favorite ______________.
바나나 파이는 Tim의 가장 좋아하는 간식이다.

4 Can you open the ______________? 창문 좀 열어줄래요?

5 Can I ______________ you a favor? 부탁 해도 될까요?

6 What is the ______________ of oranges? 오렌지는 가격이 얼마에요?

7 Jina seems to have a ______________. 지나는 문제가 있는 것처럼 보인다.

8 Do you want something to ______________? 무엇을 좀 마실래요?

9 May goes to an Italian restaurant ______________ a month.
May는 한 달에 한 번 이탈리아 식당에 간다.

10 Eunji helped her grandfather pick ______________.
은지는 할아버지께서 복숭아 따는 것을 도와드렸다.

B 빈 칸에 알맞은 단어를 고르세요.

1 The box is too ______________ for Tim.
① heavy ② goat ③ closet ④ peace ⑤ wrong

2 The ______________ of this computer is too expensive.
① ask ② house ③ business ④ second ⑤ price

3 The only ______________ for us is the weather.
① smile ② problem ③ ask ④ closet ⑤ pea

Day 18

MP3

351 **second** [sékənd]

형 두 번째의

the second of July 7월 2일
the Second World War 2차 세계 대전

352 **grow** [grou]

동 성장하다, 자라다 grow-grew-grown

grow taller 키가 커지다 grow tomatoes 토마토를 재배하다

353 **goat** [gout]

명 염소

goat's milk 염소의 우유 a mountain goat 산양

354 **house** [haus]

명 집

Amy's house Amy의 집 build a house 집을 짓다

355 **twice** [twais]

부 두 번

twice a week 일주일에 두 번 once or twice 한두 번

356 **pea** [piː]

명 완두콩

pea soup 콩 수프 a green pea 푸른 완두콩

357 **peace** [piːs]

명 평화, 평온함 형 peaceful 평화로운

world peace 세계 평화 enjoy peace 평온함을 즐기다

358 **first** [fəːrst]

명 처음, 최초, 첫째 형 처음의

at first 처음에는 for the first time 처음으로

359 **smile** [smail]

명 웃음 동 웃다 smile-smiled-smiled

a big smile 환한 미소 smile sweetly 생긋 웃다

360 **wide** [waid]

형 넓은 wide-wider-widest 명 width 너비

a wide street 넓은 거리 a wide river 넓은 강

Daily Test

| 월 일 |

A 우리말에 맞게 빈 칸에 알맞은 단어를 쓰세요.

1 My father's birthday is on the ______________ of August.
아버지의 생일은 8월 2일이다.

2 When I ______________ up, I wanted to become an actress.
내가 자랐을 때, 나는 여배우가 되고 싶었다.

3 Some farmers raise ______________ for milk.
어떤 농부들은 우유를 얻기 위해서 염소를 키운다.

4 Let's have a party at Tim's ______________. Tim의 집에서 파티를 열자.

5 Jieun and I go swimming ______________ a week.
지은과 나는 일주일에 두 번 수영을 간다.

6 Today, mom made ______________ soup for breakfast.
엄마는 오늘 아침으로 콩 수프를 만들어 주셨다.

7 We enjoyed ______________ and quiet at the beach.
우리는 해변가에서 마음의 평온함을 즐겼다.

8 I went to Hong Kong for the ______________ time last year.
작년에 난 처음으로 홍콩에 다녀왔다.

9 Hana always ______________. Hana는 항상 웃는다.

10 The window was ______________ open. 창문은 넓게 열려 있었다.

B 빈 칸에 알맞은 단어를 고르세요.

1 Today is the ______________ of March.
① one ② second ③ drink ④ once ⑤ twice

2 My grandmother ______________ red roses in her garden.
① pea ② once ③ grew ④ drank ⑤ peace

3 The river becomes ______________ from here.
① earlier ② wider ③ first ④ heavy ⑤ second

Review Test 09

Day 17 + Day 18 | 월 일 |

A 우리말에 맞게 빈 칸에 알맞은 단어를 쓰세요.

1 ________________ a week 일주일에 두 번

2 a picture on the ________________ 벽 위의 그림

3 a special ________________ 특별한 대우

4 at the ________________ 공항에서

5 by ________________ 배로

6 green ________________ 푸른 완두콩

7 ________________ a question 질문하다

8 ________________ a month 한 달에 한 번

9 the ________________ of July 7월 2일

10 for the ________________ time 처음으로

B 다음 영어 풀이에 알맞은 어휘를 〈보기〉에서 고르세요.

보기	closet	museum	snack	top	tower

1 ____________ : a small room used for storing things like clothes or dishes

2 ____________ : a light or small meal eaten between regular meals

3 ____________ : a building where important historical and artistic items are on display

4 ____________ : a tall and narrow building that stands high above the ground

5 ____________ : the highest point, side, or level of something

C 다음 단어의 관계가 A:B=C:D가 되도록 알맞은 단어를 골라 빈 칸에 적으세요.

1 sick : healthy = ______________ : see

① blind ② fire ③ watch
④ grow ⑤ touch

2 ______________ : bottom = everything : nothing

① tower ② ground ③ top
④ high ⑤ land

3 ask : price = solve : ______________

① math ② tower ③ wall
④ ship ⑤ problem

4 egg : hen = milk : ______________

① sea ② goat ③ high
④ bird ⑤ rock

5 build : ______________ = drink : water

① second ② snack ③ towel
④ house ⑤ stick

D 문맥에 맞게 다음 문장을 완성하세요.

1 My grandfather bought •
2 Will you go out •
3 I went to the National •
4 The window was •
5 When I grew up •

• a a new walking stick.
• b wide open.
• c tonight with us?
• d Science Museum last Saturday.
• e I wanted to become an actress.

E 문장을 읽고 문맥에 적절한 단어를 고르세요.

1 You should not (treat/touch) the dog. It will bark at you.

2 I need fresh air. Can you please open the (window/closet) for me?

3 I think you could buy this bike at a cheaper (snack/price) at the store.

4 I feel happy when she (smiles/paints) at me.

5 The big (fire/pea) burnt most of the mountain.

F 문장의 빈칸에 알맞은 단어를 <보기>에서 찾아 쓰세요. (필요하면 형태를 고치세요.)

보기 peace peach rock drink police

1 Cars could not move because of the big ____________ on the road.
도로에 있는 큰 바위 때문에 자동차들이 더 이상 움직일 수 없었다.

2 I like the juicy taste of ____________.
나는 과즙이 풍부한 복숭아의 맛을 좋아한다.

3 A dove is a symbol of ____________.
비둘기는 평화의 상징이다.

4 The ____________ stopped the visitors and asked questions.
경찰은 방문객들을 멈춰 세우고 질문을 했다.

5 I ____________ a glass of water when I get up in the morning.
나는 아침에 일어난 뒤 물 한잔을 마신다.

G 그림에 해당하는 낱말을 〈보기〉에서 골라 쓰세요.

1 

(　　　　　　　　)

2 

(　　　　　　　　)

3 

(　　　　　　　　)

4 

(　　　　　　　　)

5 

(　　　　　　　　)

6 

(　　　　　　　　)

보기　shoulder　towel　paint　sick　heavy　closet

Study More

see, look, 그리고 watch

- [see/look/watch] : 모두 '보다'라는 기본적 의미이나 용법상 차이점도 있다.
  see 가장 일반적인 의미의 '보다'　watch 의도적으로 지켜보다, 주시하다
  look 특정한 방향으로 보는 것(바라보다, 쳐다보다), 따라서 전치사 필요.
- [비교] : see TV (X) vs. **watch TV** (O)
  look a picture (X) vs. **look at** a picture (O)

Day 19

MP3

361 **wear** [wɛər]
동 입다 wear-wore-worn
wear a coat 코트를 입다 wear a seat belt 안전벨트를 매다

362 **shirt** [ʃəːrt]
명 셔츠
a white shirt 흰 셔츠 buy a new shirt 새 셔츠를 사다

363 **catch** [kætʃ]
동 붙잡다 catch-caught-caught
catch a horse 말을 잡다 catch a cold 감기에 걸리다

364 **pocket** [pákit]
명 주머니
a coat pocket 코트 주머니 pocket money 용돈

365 **city** [síti]
명 도시
a major city 주요 도시 city hall 시청

366 **power** [páuər]
명 힘
the power of nature 자연의 힘 a power station 발전소

367 **sit** [sit]
동 앉다 sit-sat-sat
sit down 앉다 sit on a chair 의자에 앉다

368 **week** [wiːk]
명 주
this week 이번 주 a week ago 일주일 전

369 **usually** [júːʒuəli]
부 보통, 대개 형 usual 흔히 있는, 보통의
usually go to school by bus 보통 버스를 타고 학교에 가다
usually exercise in the morning 아침에 보통 운동을 한다

370 **map** [mæp]
명 지도
draw a map 지도를 그리다 read a map 지도를 읽다

Daily Test

| 월 일 |

A 우리말에 맞게 빈 칸에 알맞은 단어를 쓰세요.

1 Bob ______________ a blue jacket. Bob은 파란 자켓을 입고 있다.

2 Jane bought a red ______________ yesterday. Jane은 어제 빨간 셔츠를 샀다.

3 Nelly ______________ the robber last week. Nelly는 지난 주에 강도를 잡았다.

4 I put the ring in my ______________. 나는 내 주머니에 반지를 넣었다.

5 Which bus goes to ______________ Hall? 어떤 버스가 시청에 갑니까?

6 The ______________ of love is great. 사랑의 힘은 위대하다.

7 Who ______________ by Alex? Alex 옆에 누가 앉아?

8 Jack will meet Junghwan next ______________. Jack은 다음 주에 정환을 만날 것이다.

9 Tim ______________ goes to bed at 10 p.m. Tim은 보통 10시에 잔다.

10 Can you find the museum on the ______________?
너 지도에서 그 박물관 찾을 수 있니?

B 빈 칸에 알맞은 단어를 고르세요.

1 Jinsu ______________ a black jacket and red shoes.
① wears ② exercises ③ cities ④ guides ⑤ words

2 ______________ down, please.
① Guide ② Sit ③ Library ④ Feel ⑤ Catch

3 Harry ______________ the ball with his left hand.
① grew ② caught ③ drank ④ sat ⑤ guided

Day 19

MP3

371 ☐ **exercise** [éksərsàiz]
명 운동 동 운동하다 exercise-exercised-exercised
take exercise 운동 하다
do exercise regularly 규칙적으로 운동하다

372 ☐ **gym** [dʒim]
명 체육관
a gym teacher 체육 선생님
play basketball in the gym 체육관에서 농구를 하다

373 ☐ **pumpkin** [pʌ́mpkin]
명 호박
pumpkin pie 호박 파이 pumpkin soup 호박 수프

374 ☐ **library** [láibrèri]
명 도서관
a school library 학교 도서관
borrow books from a library 도서관에서 책을 빌리다

375 ☐ **word** [wəːrd]
명 단어
English words 영어 단어들 in a word 간단히 말해서

376 ☐ **dictionary** [díkʃənèri]
명 사전
an English dictionary 영어 사전
look up a word in a dictionary 사전에서 단어를 찾다

377 ☐ **sometimes** [sʌ́mtàimz]
부 때때로
sometimes write a letter 가끔 편지를 쓰다
sometimes walk to school 가끔 학교에 걸어가다

378 ☐ **soap** [soup]
명 비누
a bar of soap 비누 한 개 soap bubbles 비누 거품

379 ☐ **guide** [gaid]
명 안내자, 안내(서)
a travel guide 여행 안내서 a guide dog 안내견

380 ☐ **feel** [fiːl]
동 느끼다 명 느낌 feel-felt-felt
feel sad 슬프다 feel pain 고통을 느끼다

Daily Test

| 월 일 |

A 우리말에 맞게 빈 칸에 알맞은 단어를 쓰세요.

1 I __________ twice a week. 나는 일주일에 두 번 운동한다.

2 Jisoo went to the __________ to play badminton.
지수는 배드민턴을 하기 위해 체육관에 갔다.

3 I ate __________ pie for dinner. 나는 저녁으로 호박 파이를 먹었다.

4 Yuna is studying for her science exam in the __________.
유나는 과학시험을 위해서 도서관에서 공부 하는 중이다.

5 The writer used easy __________ for children.
그 작가는 어린이들을 위해 쉬운 단어들을 사용했다.

6 I looked up the word in my __________.
나는 그 단어의 뜻을 내 사전에서 찾아보았다.

7 Lily __________ plays tennis with her father.
Lily는 때때로 그녀의 아버지와 테니스를 친다.

8 Wash your hands with __________. 비누로 손을 씻어라.

9 __________ dogs are trained to help blind people.
안내견은 시각 장애인들을 돕도록 훈련된다.

10 How do you __________ today? 오늘 기분이 어떠니?

B 빈 칸에 알맞은 단어를 고르세요.

1 This is a travel __________ for London.
① guide ② exercise ③ pocket ④ catch ⑤ word

2 I __________ pain all over my body.
① exercised ② wore ③ sat ④ felt ⑤ power

3 They __________ walk to school.
① power ② sometimes ③ wear ④ exercise ⑤ map

Day 20

MP3

381 **horse** [hɔːrs]

명 말

ride a horse 말을 타다　feed a horse 말에게 먹이를 주다

382 **race** [reis]

명 경주

win a race 경주에서 이기다　a bicycle race 자전거 경주

383 **shoe** [ʃuː]

명 신발

new shoes 새 신발　a pair of shoes 신발 한 켤레

384 **feed** [fiːd]

동 먹이를 주다, 먹이다, 먹여 키우다　feed-fed-fed

feed a cat 고양이에게 먹이를 주다
feed cows hay 소에게 건초를 먹이다

385 **holiday** [hálidèi]

명 휴일

a holiday season 휴가철
the Christmas holiday 크리스마스 휴일

386 **town** [taun]

명 마을, 소도시

in town 마을에　a small town 작은 마을

387 **afternoon** [ǽːftərnúːn]

명 오후

an afternoon nap 낮잠　in the afternoon 오후에

388 **fever** [fíːvər]

명 열, 열병

have a high fever 고열이 있다　run a fever 열이 나다

389 **cough** [kɔ(ː)f]

명 기침　동 기침하다　cough-coughed-coughed

a bad cough 심한 기침　cough loudly 크게 기침하다

390 **windy** [wíndi]

형 바람이 부는

on a windy day 바람 부는 날
It's windy today. 오늘은 바람이 분다.

Daily Test

| 월 일 |

A 우리말에 맞게 빈 칸에 알맞은 단어를 쓰세요.

1 Insu is riding a ________________. 인수는 말을 타는 중이다.

2 Who won the ________________? 누가 경주에서 이겼나요?

3 Take off your ________________. 신발을 벗으세요.

4 Do you want to ________________ the cows now? 너는 지금 소에게 먹이를 주길 원하니?

5 We take a family trip in this ________________ season.
우리는 이번 휴가철에 가족여행을 간다.

6 This ________________ is small but famous for good schools.
이 마을은 작지만 좋은 학교들로 유명하다.

7 Brian is taking an ________________ nap. Brian은 낮잠을 자는 중이다.

8 I couldn't go to the concert because I had a ________________.
난 열이 나기 때문에 콘서트에 갈 수 없었다.

9 He had a bad ________________. 그는 심한 기침을 했다.

10 Don't go outside on ________________ days. 바람 부는 날에 밖에 나가지 마라.

B 빈 칸에 알맞은 단어를 고르세요.

1 We were watching a bicycle ________________.
① race ② town ③ bend ④ energy ⑤ cough

2 When will Jack's family go on a ________________?
① feed ② windy ③ holiday ④ moment ⑤ fever

3 Do not ________________ the animal.
① shoe ② feed ③ cough ④ town ⑤ small

Day 20

MP3

391 **young** [jʌŋ]

형 어린, 젊은 young-younger-youngest

a young age 어린 나이 young people 어린 사람들

392 **old** [ould]

형 오래된, 나이 든 old-older-oldest

old people 늙은 사람들 16 years old 16살

393 **straight** [streit]

형 곧은 straight-straighter-straightest

go straight 직진 하다 a straight road 곧은 도로

394 **bend** [bend]

동 구부리다 bend-bent-bent

bend a stick 막대기를 구부리다
bend your knees 무릎을 구부리세요

395 **store** [stɔːr]

명 상점 유 shop 가게, 상점

a department store 백화점 a bookstore 서점

396 **moment** [móumənt]

명 순간

at that moment 그 때 for a moment 잠깐 동안

397 **notebook** [nóutbùk]

명 공책, 수첩

open a notebook 공책을 펴다
write in a notebook 공책에 적다

398 **energy** [énərdʒi]

명 에너지, 힘

solar energy 태양 에너지 food energy 식량 에너지

399 **festival** [féstəvəl]

명 축제

a film festival 영화 축제 hold a festival 축제를 열다

400 **fight** [fait]

동 싸우다 명 싸움 fight-fought-fought

fight with a brother 형제와 싸우다 stop a fight 싸움을 멈추다

Daily Test

| 월 일 |

A **우리말에 맞게 빈 칸에 알맞은 단어를 쓰세요.**

1 Mike is very ________________. Mike는 매우 어리다.

2 I'm 27 years ________________ this year. 나는 올해 27살이다.

3 Go ________________ and turn right. 직진해서 우회전 하세요.

4 ________________ down and touch your feet. 몸을 구부려서 발에 닿게 해라.

5 There's a big department ________________ around the corner.
길 모퉁이를 돌면 큰 백화점이 있다.

6 Could you wait a ________________, please? 잠시만 기다려 주시겠어요?

7 I need to buy some new ________________. 나는 몇 권의 새 공책을 사야 한다.

8 He's always full of ________________. 그는 항상 힘이 넘친다.

9 When you visit the music ________________, please do not bring your pets.
음악 축제에 올 때, 당신의 애완동물을 데리고 오지 마시오.

10 Two boys were ________________ over the toy.
두 명의 소년은 장난감 때문에 싸우는 중이었다.

B **빈 칸에 알맞은 단어를 고르세요.**

1 I ________________ with my sister yesterday.
① fought ② bent ③ cough ④ energy ⑤ fed

2 When I was ________________, I really wanted to become a professor.
① old ② young ③ feed ④ noon ⑤ moment

3 ________________ your arms and stretch your legs.
① Feed ② Bend ③ Store ④ Holiday ⑤ Ask

Review Test 10

Day 19 + Day 20 | 월 일 |

A 우리말에 맞게 빈 칸에 알맞은 단어를 쓰세요.

1 ________________ a coat 코트를 입다

2 the ________________ of nature 자연의 힘

3 a travel ________________ 여행 안내서

4 an English ________________ 영어 사전

5 ________________ walk to school 가끔 학교에 걸어가다

6 the Christmas ________________ 크리스마스 휴일

7 have a high ________________ 고열이 있다

8 ________________ a cat 고양이에게 먹이를 주다

9 for a ________________ 잠깐 동안

10 in a ________________ 간단히 말해서

B 다음 영어 풀이에 알맞은 어휘를 〈보기〉에서 고르세요.

보기	moment	race	gym	map	word

1 ____________ : a picture showing where different places are

2 ____________ : a place or building where people go for exercise

3 ____________ : a game or contest to see who runs faster than anyone else

4 ____________ : sounds or letters which have a meaning

5 ____________ : a very short period of time or a certain point in time

C 다음 단어의 관계가 A:B=C:D가 되도록 알맞은 단어를 골라 빈 칸에 적으세요.

1 wear : shirt = draw : ________________

① big ② drew ③ map
④ company ⑤ listen

2 ________________ : country = sit : stand

① city ② library ③ town
④ pocket ⑤ guide

3 young : old = straight : ________________

① up ② feed ③ go
④ bent ⑤ short

4 ________________ : gym = study : library

① notebook ② exercise ③ festival
④ power ⑤ week

5 wild : animal = solar : ________________

① strong ② moment ③ race
④ fever ⑤ energy

D 문맥에 맞게 다음 문장을 완성하세요.

1 Jack will meet Junghwan •	• a for her math exam in the library.
2 Yuna is studying •	• b feel today?
3 How do you •	• c please do not bring your pets.
4 Don't go outside •	• d on windy days.
5 When you visit the festival •	• e next week.

E 문장을 읽고 문맥에 적절한 단어를 고르세요.

1 You are already wet. Change your (shirt/fever) right now!

2 Just go (straight/store) to the end of this road.

3 Please take a chair and (wear/sit) down.

4 He goes to the (gym/store) everyday to do some exercise.

5 Junki bought running (stores/shoes) to run with his father.

F 문장의 빈칸에 알맞은 단어를 〈보기〉에서 찾아 쓰세요. (필요하면 형태를 고치세요.)

보기 usually pocket town soap notebook

1 I ____________ go to the bookstore on Saturday mornings.
나는 대개 토요일 아침마다 서점에 간다.

2 He always keeps a ____________ with him to write down his thoughts.
그는 자신의 생각을 적기 위해 항상 공책을 가지고 다닌다.

3 Wash your hands well with ____________.
비누로 손을 잘 씻어라.

4 The boy put a handful of candies in his ____________.
그 소년은 한 줌의 사탕을 자기 주머니에 넣었다.

5 These days many visitors come to this small ____________.
요즘에 많은 방문객들이 이 작은 마을을 찾는다.

G 그림과 낱말이 잘못 짝지어진 것을 고르세요. ·· (　　　　　　)

ⓐ

catch

ⓑ

pumpkin

ⓒ

run

ⓓ

cough

H 낱말과 어울리는 그림을 연결하세요.

1 fight •　　　　• ⓐ

2 old •　　　　• ⓑ

Study More

straight의 다양한 의미와 용법

- 동일한 형태로 형용사와 부사로 쓰인다.

[형용사] : a **straight** road 똑바른 길　　long **straight** hair 긴 직모
a **straight** talk 솔직한 이야기　　won three **straight** games 3연승을 하다

[부사] : Sumi looked **straight** into his eyes. 수미는 그의 눈을 똑바로 쳐다 보았다.

Day 21

MP3

401 **farm** [fɑːrm]
명 농장
on a farm 농장에서 an apple farm 사과 농장

402 **hospital** [háspitəl]
명 병원
be in hospital 병원에서 치료받고 있다
go to a hospital 병원에 가다

403 **follow** [fálou]
동 따르다 follow-followed-followed
Follow me! 날 따라와! follow the rule 규칙을 따르다

404 **add** [æd]
동 더하다 add-added-added
add 3 to 7 3 더하기 7 add some salt 약간의 소금을 넣다

405 **need** [niːd]
동 필요하다 need-needed-needed
need help 도움이 필요하다 need money 돈이 필요하다

406 **medicine** [médisin]
명 약
take medicine 약을 먹다 cold medicine 감기약

407 **mirror** [mírər]
명 거울
a hand mirror 손거울 look in the mirror 거울을 보다

408 **goal** [goul]
명 목표, 득점
the goal of my life 내 인생의 목표 make a goal 득점을 하다

409 **throw** [θrou]
동 던지다 throw-threw-thrown
throw a ball 공을 던지다 throw a rope 밧줄을 던지다

410 **forest** [fɔ́(ː)rist]
명 숲
in a forest 숲 속에서 a forest fire 산불

Daily Test

| 월 일 |

A 우리말에 맞게 빈 칸에 알맞은 단어를 쓰세요.

1 There are lots of animals on the ______________. 농장에는 많은 동물들이 있다.

2 Tim is in ______________. Tim은 입원 중이다.

3 We should ______________ the safety rules. 우리는 안전 규칙을 따라야 한다.

4 Inho ______________ sugar to his pancake. 인호는 그의 팬 케이크에 설탕을 더 뿌렸다.

5 We ______________ your help. 우리는 너의 도움이 필요하다.

6 Take this ______________ after each meal. 매 식사 후 이 약을 드세요.

7 Helen looked at herself in the ______________. Helen은 거울 속에 그녀 자신을 보았다.

8 Thomas scored a ______________ in the soccer match. Thomas는 축구 경기에서 득점을 했다.

9 Nick ______________ me a quick ball. Nick이 내게 빠른 공을 던졌다.

10 There are many trees in the ______________. 숲 속에 많은 나무들이 있다.

B 빈 칸에 알맞은 단어를 고르세요.

1 Peter went to a ______________.
① follow ② hospital ③ medicine ④ pillow ⑤ need

2 I can ______________ the ball 70 meters.
① find ② follow ③ need ④ throw ⑤ invite

3 ______________ me. I'll show you where the kitchen is.
① Follow ② Add ③ Turn ④ Pear ⑤ Flag

Day 21

MP3

411 **bread** [bred]

명 빵

bread and milk 빵과 우유　　a loaf of bread 빵 한 덩어리

412 **pillow** [pílou]

명 베개

on the pillow 베개 위에　　a pillow slip 베개 커버

413 **station** [stéiʃən]

명 역, 기관

a police station 경찰서　　a subway station 지하철 역

414 **pear** [pɛər]

명 배

a pear tree 배나무　　pear-shaped 배 모양의

415 **pencil** [pénsəl]

명 연필

a pencil case 필통　　write in pencil 연필로 쓰다

416 **find** [faind]

동 찾다　find-found-found

find Bob's house Bob의 집을 찾다

find the answer to the question 질문에 대한 답을 찾다

417 **flag** [flæg]

명 깃발

wave a flag 깃발을 흔들다　　lower a flag 기를 내리다

418 **flu** [flu:]

명 독감

have the flu / get the flu 독감에 걸리다　　a flu shot 독감 주사

419 **invite** [inváit]

동 초대하다　invite-invited-invited

invite for an interview 인터뷰에 초대하다

invite Nick to lunch Nick을 점심식사에 초대하다

420 **turn** [təːrn]

동 돌리다, 돌다　turn-turned-turned

turn right 오른쪽으로 돌다　　turn around 돌아서다

Daily Test

| 월 일 |

A 우리말에 맞게 빈 칸에 알맞은 단어를 쓰세요.

1 There is fresh ______________ and milk on the kitchen table. 주방 탁자 위에 갓 구운 빵과 우유가 있다.

2 The little girl is making a ______________ for her doll. 소녀는 그녀의 인형을 위해 베개를 만들고 있다.

3 There is a bus ______________ near my house. 우리 집 근처에 버스 정류장이 있다.

4 Jina planted a ______________ tree in the garden. 지나는 정원에 배나무를 심었다.

5 Write the answer with a ______________. 정답은 연필로 쓰세요.

6 I can't ______________ my car key. 내 차 키를 찾을 수 없다.

7 Many households raise the Korean national ______________ on August 15. 8월 15일에 많은 집들이 태극기를 올린다.

8 Peter's whole family got the ______________. Peter의 가족이 모두 독감에 걸렸다.

9 I want to ______________ John to my birthday party. 나는 John을 내 생일파티에 초대하고 싶다.

10 You should ______________ left at the corner. 그 모퉁이에서 왼쪽으로 돌아야 해요.

B 빈 칸에 알맞은 단어를 고르세요.

1 Hojin ______________ around to see the picture.

① turned ② found ③ thrown ④ added ⑤ goal

2 We ______________ the castle easily.

① needed ② flag ③ turned ④ fed ⑤ found

3 I ______________ only a few friends to dinner.

① find ② throw ③ invited ④ add ⑤ follow

Day 22

MP3

421 **take** [teik]

동 타다, 사진을 찍다 take-took-taken

take the subway 지하철을 타다 take a picture 사진을 찍다

422 **picture** [píktʃər]

명 그림, 사진

draw a picture 그림을 그리다

a picture of Nick's family Nick의 가족 사진

423 **pass** [pæs]

동 지나가다, 건네주다, (시험을) 통과하다 pass-passed-passed

pass his house 그의 집을 지나치다 pass a test 시험을 통과하다

424 **practice** [prǽktis]

명 연습 동 연습하다 practice-practiced-practiced

ballet practice 발레 연습 practice dance 춤을 연습하다

425 **travel** [trǽvəl]

명 여행 동 여행가다 travel-traveled-traveled

train travel 기차 여행

travel around the world 전 세계를 여행하다

426 **bee** [biː]

명 벌

a honey bee 꿀벌 a beehive 벌집, 벌통

427 **honey** [hʌ́ni]

명 꿀

honey cake 꿀 케이크 a honey jar 꿀 항아리

428 **lovely** [lʌ́vli]

형 사랑스러운, 멋진

a lovely girl 사랑스러운 소녀 look lovely 사랑스럽게 보인다

429 **bank** [bæŋk]

명 은행

go to the bank 은행에 가다 a bank teller 은행원

430 **pig** [pig]

명 돼지

raise a pig 돼지를 기르다 a piggy bank 돼지 저금통

Daily Test

| 월 일 |

A 우리말에 맞게 빈 칸에 알맞은 단어를 쓰세요.

1 He ______________ many pictures of the animals in the zoo. 동물원에 있는 동물들의 사진을 많이 찍었다.

2 A ______________ of the moon is hung on the wall. 달 그림이 벽에 걸려 있었다.

3 Could you ______________ me the sugar? 설탕 좀 건네 주시겠어요?

4 Lina ______________ the piano all day. Lina는 종일 피아노를 연습했다.

5 I want to ______________ around the world by train. 나는 기차로 전 세계를 여행하고 싶다.

6 He works like a ______________. 그는 벌처럼 일한다.

7 The bees in this farm produce a lot of ______________. 이 농장의 벌들은 많은 양의 꿀을 생산한다.

8 Look at the ______________ girl! 저 사랑스러운 소녀를 봐!

9 We can keep our money in the ______________. 우리는 은행에 돈을 맡길 수 있다.

10 ______________ hair is used to make brushes. 돼지의 털은 붓을 만드는데 쓰인다.

B 빈 칸에 알맞은 단어를 고르세요.

1 I ______________ the subway to school.

① took ② traveled ③ gave ④ spoke ⑤ practiced

2 Jenny ______________ singing for two hours every day.

① passed ② spoke ③ traveled ④ practices ⑤ found

3 Let's ______________ to Paris this winter.

① honey ② fun ③ travel ④ turn ⑤ follow

Day 22

MP3

431 **post office** [poʊst ɔ́(:)fis]

명 우체국

go to the post office 우체국에 가다
Where is the post office? 우체국이 어디에요?

432 **runny** [rʌ́ni]

형 콧물이 나는, 묽은

have a runny nose 콧물이 나다

433 **quiz** [kwiz]

명 퀴즈

a math quiz 수학 퀴즈 take a quiz 퀴즈를 치르다

434 **history** [híst∂ri]

명 역사 형 historical 역사와 관련된

a history teacher 역사 선생님
history of the Internet 인터넷의 역사

435 **fork** [fɔːrk]

명 포크

a knife and fork 칼과 포크 a salad fork 샐러드용 포크

436 **from** [frəm]

전 ~로 부터

from now on 이제부터
from Seoul to Busan 서울에서 부산까지

437 **fun** [fʌn]

형 재미있는 명 재미, 즐거움

a fun time 즐거운 시간 have fun 재미있게 놀다

438 **speak** [spiːk]

동 말하다 speak-spoke-spoken

speak English 영어를 말하다 speak loud 크게 말하다

439 **gift** [gift]

명 선물

a Christmas gift 크리스마스 선물
a gift for parents 부모님을 위한 선물

440 **give** [giv]

동 주다 give-gave-given

give a flower 꽃을 주다 give her a book 그녀에게 책을 주다

Daily Test

| 월 일 |

A 우리말에 맞게 빈 칸에 알맞은 단어를 쓰세요.

1 How can I get to the ________________? 우체국에 어떻게 가죠?

2 I have a ________________ nose. 나 지금 콧물이 나고 있어.

3 I have a math ________________ in the afternoon. 나는 오후에 수학 퀴즈가 있다.

4 Korea has a ________________ that is longer than 5,000 years.
한국은 5천년 이상의 긴 역사를 가지고 있다.

5 Western people usually eat with a knife and ________________.
서양 사람들은 보통 칼과 나이프로 식사한다.

6 Lily will travel ________________ New York to France next week.
Lily는 다음주에 뉴욕에서 프랑스까지 여행을 갈 것이다.

7 There are many ________________ things in the magic box.
마법 상자 안에는 많은 재미있는 것들이 있다.

8 Can I ________________ to Brad, please? Brad와 통화 할 수 있을까요?

9 The book is a ________________ from my grandmother.
이 책은 할머니로부터의 선물이다.

10 My mother ________________ me two movie tickets.
어머니가 내게 영화표 2장을 주셨다.

B 빈 칸에 알맞은 단어를 고르세요.

1 Where are you ________________?
① take ② bank ③ give ④ to ⑤ from

2 We will have a ________________ exam tomorrow.
① fork ② history ③ picture ④ honey ⑤ from

3 Can you ________________ English?
① travel ② take ③ speak ④ bank ⑤ give

Review Test 11

A 우리말에 맞게 빈 칸에 알맞은 단어를 쓰세요.

1 __________ Nick to lunch Nick을 점심식사에 초대하다

2 look in the __________ 거울을 보다

3 make a __________ 득점을 하다

4 on the __________ 베개 위에

5 __________ Bob's house Bob의 집을 찾다

6 __________ a picture 사진을 찍다

7 __________ dance 춤을 연습하다

8 go to the __________ 우체국에 가다

9 have a __________ nose 콧물이 나다

10 __________ Seoul to Busan 서울에서 부산까지

B 다음 영어 풀이에 알맞은 어휘를 〈보기〉에서 고르세요.

보기 quiz fork farm pencil forest

1 __________ : a place where people grow food and animals

2 __________ : a long and thin object made from wood and used for writing

3 __________ : a test with short questions and usually taken without preparation

4 __________ : a tool with two or more pointed ends used for eating food

5 __________ : a large area where many trees and other plants grow

C 다음 단어의 관계가 A:B = C:D가 되도록 알맞은 단어를 골라 빈 칸에 적으세요.

1 love : ________________ = luck : luckily

① lovely ② loved ③ lovily
④ loving ⑤ loves

2 give : gift = ________________ : English

① math ② difficult ③ speak
④ quiz ⑤ last

3 solve : ________________ = make : goal

① took ② quiz ③ mirror
④ post office ⑤ station

4 give : ________________ = go : went

① giving ② given ③ gave
④ gaved ⑤ gived

5 ________________ : farmer = hospital : doctor

① ground ② patient ③ rice
④ sick ⑤ farm

D 문맥에 맞게 다음 문장을 완성하세요.

1 There is a bus •	• a	the safety rules.
2 We should follow •	• b	station near my house.
3 The bees in this farm •	• c	in the bank.
4 We can keep our money •	• d	produce a lot of honey.
5 The book is a gift •	• e	from my grandmother.

E 문장을 읽고 문맥에 적절한 단어를 고르세요.

1 Mother likes to bake (bread/pear) at home.

2 Amy went to see a doctor to have a (flu/fun) shot.

3 I (need/add) your help to move these boxes.

4 The soup is salty. Why don't you (add/travel) some more water?

5 The road ahead is blocked. We should (throw/turn) the left.

F 문장의 빈칸에 알맞은 단어를 〈보기〉에서 찾아 쓰세요. (필요하면 형태를 고치세요.)

보기	pig	travel	history	pear	picture

1 My grandfather wants to grow ____________ trees from next year.
할아버지는 다음 해부터 배나무를 키우기 원하신다.

2 Sejin is planning to ____________ across Canada by train.
세진은 캐나다를 기차로 가로 지르는 여행을 하려고 한다.

3 He always keeps his family ____________ in his wallet.
그는 항상 지갑에 자신의 가족 사진을 가지고 다닌다.

4 We can learn a lot from ____________.
우리는 역사로부터 많은 것을 배울 수 있다.

5 ____________ have a good sense of smell.
돼지들은 좋은 후각을 가지고 있다.

G 그림에 해당하는 낱말을 〈보기〉에서 골라 쓰세요.

1 

(   )

2 

(   )

3 

(   )

4 

(   )

5 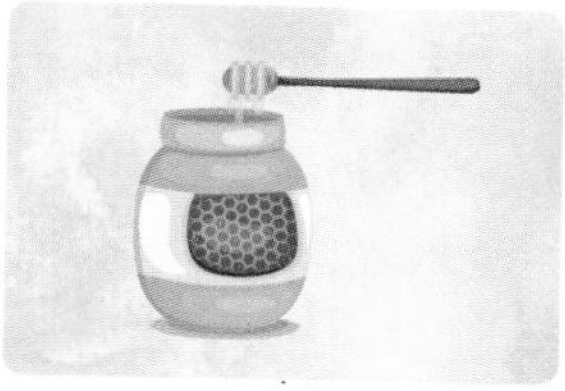

(   )

6 

(   )

보기	pass	medicine	throw	flag	honey	hospital

Study More

전치사 from의 다양한 의미

- [from A (to B)] : '~에서 (~까지)' [장소]
  Liam walked **from** home **to** school. Liam은 집에서 학교까지 걸었다.
- [be made from+명사] : '~으로 만들어지다' [재료]
  This juice **is made from** apples. 이 주스는 사과로 만들어 진다.

Day 23

MP3

441 **pair** [pɛər]
명 쌍, 켤레
a pair of earrings 한 쌍의 귀걸이　a pair of gloves 장갑 한 켤레

442 **bottle** [bátl]
명 병
a bottle of water 물 한 병　a juice bottle 주스 병

443 **stove** [stouv]
명 난로
on the stove 난로 위에　a gas stove 가스 난로

444 **magic** [mǽdʒik]
명 마법
a magic mirror 마법의 거울　the magic of love 사랑의 마법

445 **tall** [tɔːl]
형 키가 큰　tall-taller-tallest
a tall guy 키가 큰 남자　grow tall 키가 크다

446 **pink** [piŋk]
형 분홍의　명 분홍색
a pink ribbon 분홍색 리본　a pink dress 분홍색 드레스

447 **building** [bíldiŋ]
명 건물
a tall building 높은 건물　old buildings 오래된 건물들

448 **daughter** [dɔ́ːtər]
명 딸
my cute daughter 내 귀여운 딸
her wise daughter 그녀의 현명한 딸

449 **son** [sʌn]
명 아들
an only son 외동 아들　the eldest son 장남

450 **brother** [brʌ́ðər]
명 남자 형제
my little brother 내 어린 남동생　an elder brother 형

Daily Test

| 월 일 |

A 우리말에 맞게 빈 칸에 알맞은 단어를 쓰세요.

1 Minji bought a ________________ of boots. 민지는 부츠 한 켤레를 샀다.

2 A ________________ is floating on the river. 한 개의 병이 강 위에 떠 있다.

3 The kettle is boiling on the ________________. 난로 위에 주전자가 끓고 있다.

4 Do you believe in ________________? 너는 마법을 믿니?

5 My sister is ________________ and pretty. 내 여동생은 키가 크고 예쁘다.

6 This ________________ dress goes well with red shoes. 이 분홍색 치마는 빨간 구두와 잘 어울린다.

7 This ________________ is tall but old. 이 건물은 높지만 오래 되었다.

8 I have a son and three ________________. 난 한 명의 아들과 세 명의 딸이 있다.

9 Jason is the eldest ________________. Jason은 장남이다.

10 Tim likes to play with his ________________. Tim은 그의 형과 노는 것을 좋아한다.

B 빈 칸에 알맞은 단어를 고르세요.

1 There is a ________________ of apple juice on the table.
① bottle ② glue ③ stove ④ habit ⑤ hat

2 Sumin ________________ a pair of shoes yesterday.
① stove ② sounded ③ surprised ④ tall ⑤ bought

3 My ________________ is 9 years old.
① glad ② daughter ③ quiz ④ glue ⑤ grammar

Day 23

MP3

451 **have** [həv]

동 가지고 있다 have-had-had

have a new boat 새 보트를 가지고 있다 have time 시간이 있다

452 **glue** [gluː]

명 풀

a quick-drying glue 빨리 마르는 풀
put glue on paper 종이에 풀칠을 하다

453 **grade** [greid]

명 학년, 성적

be in the second grade 2학년이다
get a good grade 좋은 성적을 받다

454 **grammar** [grǽmər]

명 문법 형 grammatical 문법의, 문법에 맞는

English grammar 영어 문법 rules of grammar 문법의 규칙

455 **habit** [hǽbit]

명 습관

a good habit 좋은 습관 old habits 오랜 습관들

456 **hall** [hɔːl]

명 강당, 홀

a concert hall 콘서트 홀 City Hall 시청

457 **hamburger** [hǽmbə̀ːrgər]

명 햄버거

eat a hamburger 햄버거를 먹다
order a hamburger 햄버거를 주문하다

458 **happen** [hǽpən]

동 발생하다, 일어나다 happen-happened-happened

What happened? 무슨 일이야? happen to 우연히 ~하다

459 **hat** [hæt]

명 모자

a black hat 검은 모자 wear a hat 모자를 쓰다

460 **sister** [sístər]

명 여자 형제

a big sister 누나, 언니 a younger sister 어린 여동생

Daily Test

| 월 일 |

A 우리말에 맞게 빈 칸에 알맞은 단어를 쓰세요.

1 The man ______________ a nice boat. 그는 멋진 보트를 가지고 있었다.

2 We use ______________ to stick papers together. 우리는 종이들을 붙이기 위해 풀을 사용한다.

3 My sister is in the fifth ______________. 내 여동생은 5학년이다.

4 He teaches the basic rules of English ______________. 그는 영어 문법의 기본 규칙을 가르친다.

5 It's a good ______________ to eat breakfast. 아침을 먹는 것은 좋은 습관이다.

6 I met Andy in front of the concert ______________. 나는 Andy를 콘서트 홀 앞에서 만났다.

7 I want to eat a ______________. 나는 햄버거를 먹고 싶다.

8 I can't remember how this ______________. 나는 어떻게 이런 일이 벌어졌는지 기억나지 않는다.

9 Minsu wears a blue ______________. 민수는 파란 모자를 썼다.

10 Lily is my big ______________. Lily는 나의 큰 언니이다.

B 빈 칸에 알맞은 단어를 고르세요.

1 I ______________ a question.

① grade ② have ③ habit ④ interested ⑤happened

2 I got a good ______________ on the math exam.

① tall ② happen ③ had ④ grade ⑤ pair

3 What ______________ last night?

① liked ② habit ③ stove ④ hall ⑤ happened

Day 24

MP3

461 **interesting** [intrestiŋ]

형 재미있는, 흥미로운

an interesting movie 재미있는 영화
an interesting question 흥미로운 질문

462 **like** [laik]

동 좋아하다 like-liked-liked 반 dislike 싫어하다

like English 영어를 좋아하다
like to read books 책 읽기를 좋아하다

463 **over** [óuvər]

전 넘어서, ~위에

cross over a river 강을 건너다
children of 12 and over 12세 이상의 아이들

464 **vacation** [veikéiʃən]

명 휴가, 방학

winter vacation 겨울 방학　go on vacation 휴가를 떠나다

465 **baseball** [béisbɔ̀ːl]

명 야구

play baseball 야구를 하다　a baseball stadium 야구 경기장

466 **basketball** [bǽskitbɔ̀ːl]

명 농구

play basketball 농구를 하다　a basketball player 농구 선수

467 **year** [jiər]

명 해, 년

this year 올해　Happy new year! 행복한 새해 보내세요!

468 **trip** [trip]

명 여행

take a trip 여행 하다　a school trip 수학 여행

469 **wise** [waiz]

형 지혜로운 wise-wiser-wisest 부 wisely 현명하게

a wise student 지혜로운 학생　a wise decision 지혜로운 결정

470 **pet** [pet]

명 애완동물

a pet shop 애완동물 가게　pet food 애완동물용 사료

Daily Test

| 월 일 |

A 우리말에 맞게 빈 칸에 알맞은 단어를 쓰세요.

1 The Avengers is an ________________ movie. Avengers는 재미있는 영화다.

2 Do you ________________ spaghetti? 스파게티를 좋아하나요?

3 Mr. Park is ________________ seventy years old. Mr. Park은 70세가 넘었다.

4 How was your summer ________________? 여름방학은 어땠니?

5 There is a ________________ stadium near my house. 우리 집 근처에 야구장이 있다.

6 My brother is a ________________ player. 형은 농구 선수이다.

7 Next ________________, I will become a high school student. 다음 해에 나는 고등학생이 된다.

8 My brother went on a school ________________ yesterday. 우리 오빠는 어제 수학 여행에 갔다.

9 The boy in the story is ________________ and positive. 그 이야기에서 소년은 현명하고 긍정적이다.

10 Do you have any ________________? 애완동물이 있나요?

B 빈 칸에 알맞은 단어를 고르세요.

1 I heard an ________________ story from Jinsu.
① put ② overed ③ surprised ④ interesting ⑤ sounded

2 I went to Japan during the summer ________________.
① year ② subway ③ vacation ④ shop ⑤ hen

3 Jane wants to go on a ________________ to Jeju Island.
① hen ② baseball ③ wise ④ habit ⑤ trip

Day 24

MP3

471 **pick** [pik]

동 고르다, 줍다, 따다 pick-picked-picked

pick numbers 숫자를 고르다 pick apples 사과를 따다

472 **program** [próugræm]

명 프로그램, 계획

a TV program TV 프로그램 a training program 훈련 계획

473 **put** [put]

동 놓다, 향하게 하다 put-put-put

Put your hands up. 손을 높이 들어라.
Put your coat under the chair. 코트를 의자 밑에 두어라.

474 **subway** [sʌ́bwèi]

명 지하철

a subway station 지하철 역 take the subway 지하철을 타다

475 **sure** [ʃuər]

형 확신하는

Are you sure? 확실하니? be sure of ~에 확신을 가지다

476 **surprise** [sərpráiz]

명 놀라운 일 동 놀라게하다 surprise-surprised-surprised

a surprise party 깜짝 파티 What a surprise! 놀라워라!

477 **sound** [saund]

명 소리 동 ~처럼 들리다 sound-sounded-sounded

make a sound 소리를 내다 sounds strange 이상하게 들린다

478 **health** [helθ]

명 건강 형 healthy 건강한

good for your health 당신의 건강에 좋은
take care of your health 당신의 건강을 돌보다

479 **hen** [hen]

명 암탉

raise hens 암탉을 키우다 a hen's egg 달걀

480 **here** [hiər]

부 여기에

Here you are. 여기 있어요 Come over here. 이리 오세요.

Daily Test

| 월 일 |

A 우리말에 맞게 빈 칸에 알맞은 단어를 쓰세요.

1 ______________ out whatever you want. 네가 원하는 것을 골라보렴.

2 What's your favorite TV ______________? 네가 가장 좋아하는 TV 프로그램은 무엇이니?

3 ______________ these books on the table. 이 책들을 탁자 위에 두어라.

4 Ann takes the ______________ twice a week. Ann은 일주일에 두 번 지하철을 탄다.

5 James is ______________ of victory. James는 승리를 확신했다.

6 I was ______________ at the news yesterday. 나는 어제 그 소식에 놀랐다.

7 It ______________ great! 그거 좋구나!

8 Kimchi is good for your ______________. 김치는 건강에 좋다.

9 ______________ like to bathe with dust. 암탉은 흙먼지로 목욕하기를 좋아한다.

10 We arrived ______________ at 5pm. 우리는 오후 5시에 이 곳에 도착했다.

B 빈 칸에 알맞은 단어를 고르세요.

1 ______________ your hands up if you need more food.

① Like ② Over ③ Pick ④ Down ⑤ Put

2 Are you ______________ about that?

① hen ② sure ③ put ④ pillow ⑤ old

3 Mia's voice ______________ lovely.

① sounded ② surprised ③ talked ④ sure ⑤ put

A 우리말에 맞게 빈 칸에 알맞은 단어를 쓰세요.

1 Happy new ________________! 새해 복 많이 받으세요!

2 her wise ________________ 그녀의 현명한 딸

3 a good ________________ 좋은 습관

4 What ________________? 무슨 일이야?

5 ________________ time 시간이 있다

6 an ________________ question 흥미로운 질문

7 play ________________ 야구를 하다

8 take a ________________ 여행 하다

9 make a ________________ 소리를 내다

10 Come over ________________ 이리 오세요

B 다음 영어 풀이에 알맞은 어휘를 〈보기〉에서 고르세요.

보기 hall hamburger hen pet stove

1 ____________ : a device that uses electricity, gas, or wood to make heat

2 ____________ : a large room for meetings or events

3 ____________ : a round sandwich with meat or vegetables in it

4 ____________ : an animal that you keep in your home for pleasure

5 ____________ : an adult female chicken, which lays eggs

C 다음 단어의 관계가 A:B=C:D가 되도록 알맞은 단어를 골라 빈 칸에 적으세요.

1 wise : ______________ = funny : funniest

① wiser ② wisest ③ wises
④ wised ⑤ wisested

2 ______________ : shoes = bottle : milk

① beautiful ② two ③ piece
④ pair ⑤ black

3 tall : ______________ = wide : river

① tallest ② car ③ building
④ jump ⑤ bag

4 magic : ______________ = dance : dancer

① magical ② musician ③ magics
④ magicked ⑤ magician

5 ______________ : dog = country : Korea

① pet ② cat ③ white
④ feed ⑤ care

D 문맥에 맞게 다음 문장을 완성하세요.

1	James is	a	your summer vacation?
2	He teaches	b	twice a week.
3	How was	c	the basic rules of English grammar.
4	What's your	d	favorite TV program?
5	Ann takes the subway	e	sure of victory.

E **문장을 읽고 문맥에 적절한 단어를 고르세요.**

1 I fixed the stamp to the envelope with (grade/glue).

2 The man took off his (hat/habit) and greeted the audience.

3 The horse jumped (over/sure) the fence and ran away.

4 He (sounded/put) a memo on the kitchen table before going out.

5 Everybody was (surprised/picked) to hear the news last night.

F **문장의 빈칸에 알맞은 단어를 〈보기〉에서 찾아 쓰세요. (필요하면 형태를 고치세요.)**

보기	health	pink	pick	tall	grade

1 Kate takes very good care of her ____________.
Kate는 자신의 건강을 열심히 돌본다.

2 Who is the ____________ person in your class?
너희 반에서 가장 키가 큰 사람은 누구니?

3 Darcy got a good ____________ in writing.
Darcy는 작문에서 좋은 점수를 받았다.

4 Changmin bought a bunch of ____________ roses for his mother.
창민은 어머니를 위해 한 다발의 분홍색 장미꽃을 샀다.

5 Jimin bent down to ____________ up a ring from the floor.
지민은 바닥에 있는 반지를 줍기 위해 허리를 굽혔다.

G 그림과 낱말이 <u>잘못</u> 짝지어진 것을 고르세요. ·· (   )

ⓐ

bottle

ⓑ

grade

ⓒ

son

ⓓ

basketball

H 낱말과 어울리는 그림을 연결하세요.

1 hen •

• ⓐ 

2 like •

• ⓑ 

Study More

pick의 다양한 의미

- [pick] : '고르다, 따다, 줍다'
  pick flowers 꽃을 따다 **pick** the right answer 정답을 고르다
- [pick someone up] [pick up someone] : '~를 (차로) 데리러/태우러 가다'
  My father came to the park to **pick us up.** 아버지는 우리를 데리러 공원에 오셨다.

Day 25

MP3

481 **kind** [kaind]

형 친절한 명 종류

a kind teacher 친절한 선생님 a kind of dance 춤의 한 종류

482 **great** [greit]

형 좋은, 훌륭한 great-greater-greatest

a great leader 훌륭한 지도자

have a great time 좋은 시간을 보내다

483 **little** [lítl]

형 작은, 어린 little-less-least

a little house 작은 집 my little brother 내 어린 남동생

484 **lesson** [lésən]

명 수업, 교훈

review lessons 수업을 복습하다

take a piano lesson 피아노 수업을 받다

485 **plastic** [plǽstik]

형 플라스틱으로 된 명 플라스틱

a plastic bag 비닐 봉지

a cup made of plastic 플라스틱으로 만들어진 컵

486 **shop** [ʃɑp]

명 가게 유 store 상점, 가게

a flower shop 꽃가게 a shoe shop 신발 가게

487 **society** [səsáiəti]

명 사회 형 social 사회적인

modern society 현대사회 social problems 사회적 문제

488 **hope** [houp]

동 희망하다 명 희망 hope-hoped-hoped

hope for the best 최선을 희망하다 lose hope 희망을 잃다

489 **cut** [kʌt]

동 자르다 cut-cut-cut

cut down a tree 나무를 베다

cut an orange in half 오렌지를 반으로 자르다

490 **onion** [ʌ́njən]

명 양파

onion soup 양파 수프 chop an onion 양파를 다지다

Daily Test

| 월 일 |

A 우리말에 맞게 빈 칸에 알맞은 단어를 쓰세요.

1 You can see many ______________ of flowers in the festival. 축제에서 많은 종류의 꽃들을 볼 수 있다.

2 I had a ______________ time with my family. 나는 가족들과 좋은 시간을 보냈다.

3 I should take care of my ______________ sister tonight. 나는 오늘 밤 내 어린 여동생을 돌봐야 한다.

4 Amy is taking a Chinese ______________. Amy는 중국어 교습을 받는 중이다.

5 This cup is made of ______________. 이 컵은 플라스틱으로 만들어졌다.

6 Where is the flower ______________ around here? 이 근처에 꽃가게가 어디에 있습니까?

7 Jina's favorite subject is ______________ studies. Jina의 좋아하는 과목은 사회이다.

8 I ______________ to see you tomorrow. 내일 널 보길 바랄게.

9 Hyerin ______________ a piece of birthday cake. 혜린은 생일 케이크를 한 조각 잘랐다.

10 My favorite food is ______________ soup. 내가 가장 좋아하는 음식은 양파 수프다.

B 빈 칸에 알맞은 단어를 고르세요.

1 ______________ the apple pie in half.

① Hope ② Cut ③ Hit ④ Hold ⑤ Hurt

2 John is taking guitar ______________.

① lessons ② mail ③ husband ④ shop ⑤ idea

3 There are many ______________ problems these days.

① society ② social ③ shop ④ send ⑤ kind

Day 25

MP3

491 **mail** [meil]

명 편지, 우편

a voice mail 음성 우편 　 mail service 우편 서비스

492 **send** [send]

동 보내다 　 send-sent-sent

send a postcard 엽서를 보내다
send a message 메시지를 보내다

493 **hike** [haik]

동 도보 여행을 하다 　 hike-hiked-hiked

go hiking 도보여행을 가다
hike in the mountains 산에서 하이킹을 하다

494 **hit** [hit]

동 때리다, 치다 　 hit-hit-hit

hit the target 목표를 맞추다
hit a ball with a racket 라켓으로 공을 치다

495 **hold** [hould]

동 잡고 있다, 열다 　 hold-held-held

hold hands 손을 잡다 　 hold a party 파티를 열다

496 **hometown** [hóumtáun]

명 고향

my hometown 내 고향 　 hometown friends 고향 친구

497 **hundred** [hʌ́ndrəd]

명 백

hundreds of 수백의 　 hundreds of people 수백 명의 사람들

498 **hurt** [həːrt]

동 다치다 　 형 아픈 　 hurt-hurt-hurt

hurt one's back 등을 다치다 　 a hurt leg 다친 다리

499 **husband** [hʌ́zbənd]

명 남편

a good husband 좋은 남편 　 Linda's husband Linda의 남편

500 **idea** [aidí(:)ə]

명 생각 　 형 ideal 이상적인

have an idea ~할 생각이 있다 　 a good idea 좋은 생각

Daily Test

| 월 일 |

A 우리말에 맞게 빈 칸에 알맞은 단어를 쓰세요.

1 I left a voice ________________ for James. 나는 James에게 음성 우편을 남겼다.

2 I ________________ a message to my mother. 나는 엄마께 메시지를 보냈다.

3 Alex and I will go ________________ this weekend. Alex와 나는 이번 주말에 하이킹을 갈 것이다.

4 The car ________________ the wall. 자동차가 벽을 쳤다.

5 Ann is ________________ a large box. Ann은 큰 상자를 들고 있다.

6 Gwangju is my ________________. 광주는 내 고향이다.

7 There are ________________ of people in the concert hall. 콘서트 홀에 수백 명의 사람들이 있다.

8 Sam ________________ his arm. Sam은 그의 팔을 다쳤다.

9 My ________________ likes to go fishing. 내 남편은 낚시 가는 것을 좋아한다.

10 Your ________________ is great. 너의 생각은 훌륭하다.

B 빈 칸에 알맞은 단어를 고르세요.

1 Jack's ________________ is London.
① hometown ② society ③ idea ④ kind ⑤ lesson

2 Alex ________________ his leg playing soccer.
① sounded ② sent ③ hurt ④ fought ⑤ hiked

3 Mother ________________ my hand tightly.
① kind ② held ③ hurt ④ hiked ⑤ kicked

Day 26

MP3

501 □ **life** [laif]
명 삶, 인생
my school life 나의 학교 생활 family life 가정 생활

502 □ **sheep** [ʃiːp]
명 양 복 sheep
a flock of sheep 양떼 a lost sheep 길 잃은 양

503 □ **mistake** [mistéik]
명 실수
make a mistake 실수를 하다 a terrible mistake 심각한 실수

504 □ **street** [striːt]
명 거리
across the street 길 건너 a busy street 번화가

505 □ **camel** [kǽməl]
명 낙타
ride a camel 낙타를 타다 feed a camel 낙타에게 먹이를 주다

506 □ **lake** [leik]
명 호수
in a lake 호수에서 a big lake 큰 호수

507 □ **blow** [blou]
동 불다 blow-blew-blown
blow hard 세게 불다 blow a whistle 호루라기를 불다

508 □ **balloon** [bəlúːn]
명 풍선
a big balloon 큰 풍선 blow up a balloon 풍선을 불다

509 □ **answer** [ǽnsər]
명 답, 대답 동 답하다 answer-answered-answered
find an answer 답을 찾다
answer a question 질문에 답하다

510 □ **kid** [kid]
명 아이
a little kid 어린 아이 a smart kid 현명한 아이

Daily Test

| 월 일 |

A 우리말에 맞게 빈 칸에 알맞은 단어를 쓰세요.

1 Larry talked with his parents about his school ______________.
Larry는 부모님과 그의 학교 생활에 대해 얘기를 나눴다.

2 There is a flock of ______________ on the grass. 잔디밭에 한 무리의 양이 있다.

3 Tim made a terrible ______________. Tim은 심각한 실수를 저질렀다.

4 He walked toward the main ______________. 그는 중심가를 향해 걸었다.

5 A ______________ can live long without water. 낙타는 물 없이도 오래 살 수 있다.

6 We swam in the ______________. 우리는 호수에서 수영을 했다.

7 The wind is ______________ hard. 바람이 세게 불고 있다.

8 Sarah is holding a red ______________. Sarah는 빨간 풍선을 들고 있다.

9 I found the ______________ in this book. 나는 이 책에서 정답을 알아냈다.

10 Amy is a bright ______________. Amy는 밝은 아이다.

B 빈 칸에 알맞은 단어를 고르세요.

1 Tim dropped his mother's plate by ______________.
① question ② come ③ mistake ④ joke ⑤ knee

2 Write your ______________ on this paper.
① just ② know ③ life ④ answer ⑤ print

3 The referee ______________ his whistle.
① answered ② blew ③ lake ④ knew ⑤ joked

Day 26

MP3

511 **come** [kʌm]

동 오다 come-came-come

come home 집에 오다
come from Seoul 서울에서부터 오다

512 **print** [print]

동 인쇄하다 명 인쇄물, 인쇄 print-printed-printed

print a document 문서를 인쇄하다 a color print 컬러사진/인쇄

513 **island** [áilənd]

명 섬

Jeju Island 제주도 a deserted island 무인도

514 **joke** [dʒouk]

명 농담 동 놀리다 joke-joked-joked

play a joke 장난을 치다
joke about his drawing 그의 그림에 대해 농담하다

515 **just** [dʒʌst]

부 막, 단지

just a little 단지 조금 just a moment 잠깐

516 **question** [kwéstʃən]

명 질문

ask a question 질문 하다 answer a question 질문에 답하다

517 **knee** [niː]

명 무릎

on your knee 무릎 위에
bend your knees 무릎을 구부리다

518 **knit** [nit]

동 뜨다, 짜다 knit-knitted-knitted

knit a sweater 스웨터를 짜다 knit socks 양말을 짜다

519 **know** [nou]

동 알다 know-knew-known

know his name 그의 이름을 알다
know how to ski 스키 타는 법을 알다

520 **lady** [léidi]

명 숙녀

The First Lady 영부인 ladies and gentleman 신사숙녀

Daily Test

| 월 일 |

A 우리말에 맞게 빈 칸에 알맞은 단어를 쓰세요.

1 My daughter will ______________ home next week.
내 딸은 다음주에 집에 올 것이다.

2 Alex tried to ______________ his picture. Alex는 그의 사진을 인쇄하려고 했다.

3 In spring, many people visit Jeju ______________.
봄이 되면, 많은 사람들이 제주도를 방문한다.

4 He said it only as a ______________. 그는 단지 농담으로 그 말을 했을 뿐이야.

5 We ______________ got married. 우리는 지금 막 결혼했어요.

6 May I ask you a ______________? 질문 해도 될까요?

7 She put a bandage on her ______________. 그녀는 무릎에 반창고를 붙였다.

8 Grandmother likes to ______________ sweaters.
할머니는 스웨터를 짜는 것을 좋아하신다.

9 I ______________ what you are talking about. 나는 네가 무엇을 말하는 지 알고 있다.

10 The ______________ at the desk will interview you.
저 책상에 앉아있는 여자분이 널 인터뷰 할 거야.

B 빈 칸에 알맞은 단어를 고르세요.

1 Here ______________ the bus!
① comes ② printed ③ jokes ④ just ⑤ blew

2 The math teacher kindly answered my ______________.
① knee ② joke ③ mistake ④ question ⑤ knit

3 I don't ______________ how to knit a sweater.
① come ② blow ③ mistake ④ island ⑤ know

Review Test 13

A 우리말에 맞게 빈 칸에 알맞은 단어를 쓰세요.

1 a ________________ of dance 춤의 한 종류

2 review ________________ 수업을 복습하다

3 a voice ________________ 음성 편지

4 family ________________ 가정생활

5 have an ________________ ~할 생각이 있다

6 make a ________________ 실수를 하다

7 ________________ hard 세게 불다

8 feed a ________________ 낙타에게 먹이를 주다

9 ________________ a sweater 스웨터를 짜다

10 ________________ how to ski 스키 타는 법을 알다

B 다음 영어 풀이에 알맞은 어휘를 〈보기〉에서 고르세요.

보기	island	shop	hike	hit	plastic

1 ____________ : a man-made material that can be easily shaped for many products

2 ____________ : a building or room where people can buy things

3 ____________ : to take a long walk for exercise or pleasure

4 ____________ : to touch hard against something or to strike something

5 ____________ : an area or piece of land surrounded by water

C 다음 단어의 관계가 A:B=C:D가 되도록 알맞은 단어를 골라 빈 칸에 적으세요.

1 blow : balloon = answer : ______________

① question ② golves ③ program
④ subway ⑤ sound

2 little : ______________ = big : bigger

① littler ② least ③ lesser
④ littless ⑤ less

3 cut : onion = ______________ : mail

① letter ② radio ③ send
④ post office ⑤ pink

4 come : ______________ = print : printed

① come ② comed ③ camed
④ came ⑤ comes

5 modern : ______________ = best : hope

① socials ② society ③ societied
④ societys ⑤ socialed

D 문맥에 맞게 다음 문장을 완성하세요.

1 Hyerin cut •	• a a piece of birthday cake.
2 There are hundreds of people •	• b a bright kid.
3 He walked •	• c in the concert hall.
4 We just •	• d toward the main street.
5 Amy is •	• e got married.

E 문장을 읽고 문맥에 적절한 단어를 고르세요.

1 Jerry can't walk now because he (hurt/hiked) his leg yesterday.

2 Kyoungmin likes to go (hitting/hiking) in the mountain.

3 She (joked/printed) a copy of her essay for her teacher.

4 These cups are made from (plastic/mail).

5 Derek's (joke/island) made everyone in the class laugh.

F 문장의 빈칸에 알맞은 단어를 〈보기〉에서 찾아 쓰세요. (필요하면 형태를 고치세요.)

보기	onion	sheep	hometown	leader	husband

1 The farmer raises ____________ and goats in his farm.
그 농부는 자신의 농장에서 양과 염소를 키운다.

2 I want to know how to cut an ____________ without tears.
나는 양파를 눈물을 흘리지 않고 자를 수 있는 방법을 알고 싶다.

3 He misses his ____________ where his parents and friends live.
그는 자신의 부모님과 친구들이 살고 있는 고향을 그리워한다.

4 Alice's ____________ promised to do the dishes on weekends.
Alice의 남편은 주말에는 자신이 설거지를 하기로 약속했다.

5 A great ____________ knows how to read other people's minds.
훌륭한 지도자는 다른 사람의 마음을 읽을 줄 안다.

G **그림에 해당하는 낱말을 〈보기〉에서 골라 쓰세요.**

1

(   )

2

(   )

3

(   )

4

(   )

5

(   )

6

(   )

보기 hold answer hit knee lady hope

Study More

sheep or sheeps? 단수형과 복수형이 같은 단어들

- a sheep vs. many **sheep**(양) a deer vs. many **deer**(사슴) a fish vs. many **fish**(물고기) a salmon vs. many **salmon**(연어) a trout vs. many **trout**(송어) *주로 물고기 이름들
- -craft로 끝나는 단어들 : an aircraft vs. many **aircraft** a spacecraft vs. many **spacecraft**(우주선) a hovercraft vs. many **hovercraft**(공기 부양정)

Day 27

MP3

521 **count** [kaunt]

동 세다 count-counted-counted

count up to 20 20까지 세다
count down 수를 큰 것부터 거꾸로 세다

522 **number** [nʌ́mbər]

명 숫자

a uniform number 등 번호
Mom's phone number 엄마의 전화번호

523 **taste** [teist]

명 맛 동 맛보다, 맛이 나다 taste-tasted-tasted

a salty taste 짠 맛 taste food 음식을 맛보다

524 **miss** [mis]

동 놓치다 miss-missed-missed

miss a train 기차를 놓치다
miss a good chance 좋은 기회를 놓치다

525 **member** [mémbər]

명 회원

a member of a dance club 댄스 동아리 회원
a member of a baseball club 야구 동호회 회원

526 **glad** [glæd]

형 기쁜

be glad to+동사원형 ~해서 기쁘다
be glad to help young people 젊은 사람들을 돕게 되서 기쁘다

527 **weigh** [wei]

동 무게를 재다, 무게가 나가다 weigh-weighed-weighed

weigh sugar 설탕의 무게를 재다
weigh 20 kilograms 무게가 20 킬로그램이다

528 **serve** [səːrv]

동 제공하다 serve-served-served

serve a meal 식사를 대접하다
serve lunch to the guests 손님들에게 점심을 대접하다

529 **yesterday** [jéstərdi]

명, 부 어제

yesterday morning 어제 아침
arrived yesterday 어제 도착했다

530 **high** [hai]

형 높은 부 높이 high-higher-highest

a high mountain 높은 산 a high price 높은 가격

Daily Test

| 월 일 |

A 우리말에 맞게 빈 칸에 알맞은 단어를 쓰세요.

1 Let's ________________ up to 100. 100까지 세보자.

2 His uniform ________________ is 24. 그의 등 번호는 24이다.

3 The cook ________________ his new dish. 그 요리사는 자신의 새로운 요리를 맛 보았다.

4 I ________________ the last train to Suwon. 나는 수원으로 가는 막차를 놓쳤다.

5 Wendy wants to be a ________________ of the school band. Wendy는 학교 밴드의 회원이 되길 원한다.

6 I'm ________________ to meet you. 당신을 만나서 기쁩니다.

7 How much do you ________________? 몸무게가 얼마나 나가니?

8 Mina ________________ dinner to the guests. Mina는 손님들에게 저녁을 대접했다.

9 Where did they go ________________ morning? 그들은 어제 아침에 어디에 갔니?

10 A balloon is flying ________________. 풍선은 높이 날아 가고 있다.

B 빈 칸에 알맞은 단어를 고르세요.

1 Woojin ________________ the number of new words on the page.
① counted ② weighed ③ served ④ spelled ⑤ left

2 This pasta ________________ good.
① delicious ② tastes ③ missed ④ knew ⑤ main

3 Suyoung ________________ fifty kilograms.
① misses ② spells ③ finds ④ weighs ⑤ counts

Day 27

MP3

531 **people** [píːpl]
명 사람들
common people 일반 사람들, 서민
the people of Mexico 멕시코 국민

532 **oil** [ɔil]
명 기름
olive oil 올리브 오일　an oil lamp 기름 램프

533 **later** [léitər]
부 후에, 나중에
three days later 3일 후에　See you later. 나중에 보자.

534 **spell** [spel]
동 철자를 쓰다　spell-spelled-spelled
spell a word 단어의 철자를 쓰다
learn to spell 철자를 쓰는 법을 배우다

535 **learn** [ləːrn]
동 배우다　learn-learned-learned
learn to swim 수영하는 법을 배우다
learn a foreign language 외국어를 배우다

536 **leave** [liːv]
동 떠나다, 출발하다　leave-left-left
leave a room 방을 나가다　leave for Busan 부산으로 가다

537 **magazine** [mæ̀gəzíːn]
명 잡지
a fashion magazine 패션 잡지
a monthly magazine 월간 잡지

538 **main** [mein]
형 주요한, 주된　부 mainly 주로
a main idea 주제　a main character 주인공

539 **many** [méni]
형 많은
many friends 많은 친구들　many years 수년, 여러 해

540 **market** [máːrkit]
명 시장
go to the market 장 보러 가다　a flower market 꽃 시장

Daily Test

A **우리말에 맞게 빈 칸에 알맞은 단어를 쓰세요.**

1 There were already many ______________ in the park.
공원에는 이미 많은 사람들이 있었다.

2 Put some olive ______________ in the salad. 샐러드에 올리브 오일을 좀 넣어라.

3 We will go to the amusement park three days ______________.
우리는 3일 뒤에 놀이동산에 갈 것이다.

4 How do you ______________ your name, Junsu? 준수, 너의 이름은 어떻게 써?

5 Jane wants to ______________ to swim. Jane은 수영 하는 법을 배우고 싶다.

6 She will ______________ for Busan tomorrow. 그녀는 내일 부산으로 떠날 것이다.

7 Would you like to read a ______________? 잡지를 보시겠어요?

8 What is the ______________ idea of this book? 이 책의 주제는 무엇인가요?

9 ______________ tourists visit this village. 많은 관광객들이 이 마을을 방문한다.

10 Mary bought some oranges at the ______________.
Mary는 시장에서 오렌지를 몇 개 샀다.

B **빈 칸에 알맞은 단어를 고르세요.**

1 He started to ______________ Hangul, the Korean Alphabet.
① learn ② main ③ count ④ later ⑤ off

2 She ______________ the room.
① off ② weigh ③ served ④ main ⑤ left

3 I have ______________ candies.
① much ② many ③ miss ④ leave ⑤ eat

Day 28

MP3

541 **think** [θiŋk]

동 생각하다 think-thought-thought

think about ~에 대해 생각하다
think about the future 미래에 대해 생각하다

542 **cover** [kʌ́vər]

동 덮다, 가리다 명 덮개, 표지 cover-covered-covered

cover your eyes 눈을 가리다 on the book cover 책 표지 위에

543 **each** [iːtʃ]

형 각각의 대 각각

each other 서로 each country 각각의 나라

544 **all** [ɔːl]

형 모든 대 모두

all year round 일년 내내 all of us 우리 모두

545 **start** [stɑːrt]

동 시작하다 start-started-started

start a new job 새로운 일을 시작하다
start work at eight 8시에 일을 시작하다

546 **finish** [fíniʃ]

동 마치다 finish-finished-finished

finish a race 경주를 마치다 finish school 학업을 마치다

547 **angel** [éindʒəl]

명 천사

a little angel 작은 천사 like an angel 천사와 같이

548 **hurry** [hə́ːri]

동 서두르다 명 서두름, 급함 hurry-hurried-hurried

Hurry up! 서둘러! in a hurry 서둘러, 황급히

549 **say** [sei]

동 말하다 say-said-said

say hello to ~에게 안부를 묻다
say something in Chinese 중국어로 무언가 말하다

550 **simple** [símpl]

형 간단한 simple-simpler-simplest

a simple design 간결한 디자인
a simple question 간단한 질문

Daily Test

| 월 일 |

A 우리말에 맞게 빈 칸에 알맞은 단어를 쓰세요.

1 What do you ________________ about this picture? 이 사진에 대해 어떻게 생각하니?

2 ________________ your eyes and count to 10. 눈을 가리고 10까지 세시오.

3 ________________ student needs to write a report. 각 학생들은 보고서를 써야 한다.

4 It was raining ________________ day. 하루 종일 비가 오고 있었다.

5 The math exam ________________ at ten. 수학 시험은 10시에 시작했다.

6 Bob was happy to ________________ his homework. Bob은 그의 숙제를 끝내서 행복했다.

7 She looks like an ________________. 그녀는 천사같이 보인다.

8 Mina ________________ to catch the train. 미나는 기차를 타기 위해 서둘렀다.

9 Max ________________ hello to his grandmother. Max는 그의 할머니께 안부를 물었다.

10 The melody of the song is very ________________. 그 노래의 멜로디는 아주 간단하다.

B 빈 칸에 알맞은 단어를 고르세요.

1 The concert ________________ on time.

① covered ② went ③ started ④ marry ⑤ may

2 She ________________ that Jina was kind and humorous.

① match ② cover ③ welcome ④ started ⑤ thought

3 It's not a ________________ problem.

① hurry ② simple ③ every ④ cover ⑤ match

Day 28

MP3

551 **weekend** [wíːkènd]

명 주말

last weekend 지난 주말　　on the weekend 주말에

552 **welcome** [wélkəm]

형 환영하는　동 환영하다　welcome-welcomed-welcomed

a welcome party 환영 파티
welcome new students 새로운 학생들을 환영하다

553 **every** [évri]

형 모든

every person 모든 사람　　every morning 매일 아침

554 **letter** [létər]

명 편지

write a letter 편지를 쓰다　　send a letter 편지를 보내다

555 **hill** [hil]

명 언덕, (나지막한) 산, 경사로

a steep hill 가파른 언덕　　downhill 비탈 아래로

556 **marry** [mǽri]

동 ~와 결혼하다　marry-married-married

marry a Korean person 한국인과 결혼하다
get married to a nurse 간호사와 결혼하다

557 **mask** [mæsk]

명 가면

wear a mask 가면을 쓰다　　party masks 파티용 가면

558 **match** [mætʃ]

명 경기

a basketball match 농구 경기
win a baseball match 야구경기에서 이기다

559 **matter** [mǽtər]

명 문제

a serious matter 심각한 문제
What's the matter? 무슨 일이야?

560 **may** [mei]

조 ~해도 좋다

May I help you? 도와드릴까요?
May I come in? 들어가도 되나요?

Daily Test

| 월 일 |

A 우리말에 맞게 빈 칸에 알맞은 단어를 쓰세요.

1 Have a good ________________! 좋은 주말 보내세요!

2 ________________ to my house. 우리 집에 오신 것을 환영합니다.

3 My father reads a newspaper ________________ morning.
아버지는 매일 아침 신문을 읽으신다.

4 Whose ________________ is that? 저것은 누구의 편지니?

5 Please be careful when you drive down the ________________.
경사로를 운전하여 내려갈 때 제발 조심 하거라.

6 Will you ________________ me? 나와 결혼 해 줄래요?

7 Brad wore a ________________ and started dusting the rooms.
Brad는 마스크를 쓰고 방들의 먼지를 털기 시작했다.

8 Our tennis team won the final ________________. 우리 테니스 팀은 결승전에서 우승했다.

9 What is the ________________ with you? 무슨 문제가 있나요?

10 ________________ I use your camera? 당신의 카메라를 써도 될 까요?

B 빈 칸에 알맞은 단어를 고르세요.

1 Mr. and Mrs. Smith ________________ us warmly.
① every ② weekend ③ welcomed ④ match ⑤ may

2 James ________________ an American lady.
① said ② married ③ weekend ④ matter ⑤ came

3 What's the ________________ with Liam? He looks worried.
① joke ② marry ③ finish ④ simple ⑤ matter

Review Test 14

Day 27 + Day 28 | 월 일 |

A 우리말에 맞게 빈 칸에 알맞은 단어를 쓰세요.

1 ________________ up to 20 20까지 세다

2 ________________ a train 기차를 놓치다

3 ________________ sugar 설탕의 무게를 재다

4 ________________ to swim 수영하는 법을 배우다

5 be ________________ to help young people 젊은 사람들을 돕게 되서 기쁘다

6 ________________ other 서로

7 in a ________________ 서둘러, 황급히

8 a ________________ party 환영 파티

9 ________________ a Korean person 한국인과 결혼하다

10 take your hat ________________ 모자를 벗다

B 다음 영어 풀이에 알맞은 어휘를 〈보기〉에서 고르세요.

보기	weekend	number	every	magazine	letter

1 ____________ : a word or symbol that we use for counting things

2 ____________ : the end of a week: Saturday and Sunday

3 ____________ : a message written on paper and sent to another person

4 ____________ : a kind of book that comes out regularly with stories and news

5 ____________ : each and all parts or members in a group of people or things

C 다음 단어의 관계가 A:B=C:D가 되도록 알맞은 단어를 골라 빈 칸에 적으세요.

1 today : ________________ = on : off

① yesterday ② last ③ night
④ day ⑤ week

2 ________________ : thought = cover : covered

① thinks ② thinked ③ thinking
④ thinker ⑤ think

3 start : ________________ = angel : devil

① begin ② finish ③ run
④ back ⑤ later

4 count : number = ________________ : soup

① tasty ② delicious ③ good
④ taste ⑤ rest

5 read : ________________ = bake : pie

① run ② sky ③ magazine
④ victory ⑤ road

D 문맥에 맞게 다음 문장을 완성하세요.

1	Wendy wants to be •	• a	at the market.
2	Mina served •	• b	your name, Junsu?
3	How do you spell •	• c	dinner to the guests.
4	Mary bought some oranges •	• d	to his grandmother.
5	Max said hello •	• e	a member of the school band.

E 문장을 읽고 문맥에 적절한 단어를 고르세요.

1 (May/Glad) I ask you a favor?

2 I think it is too early to talk about it. Let us talk about it (later/off).

3 He wanted to call his sister but forgot his sister's phone (cover/number).

4 The whole mountain is now (covered/missed) by snow.

5 She was (all/glad) to be home again and living with her family.

F 문장의 빈칸에 알맞은 단어를 <보기>에서 찾아 쓰세요. (필요하면 형태를 고치세요.)

보기	main	mask	simple	oil	matter

1 It took him two hours to write a ____________ email message.
그가 간단한 이메일 메시지 하나를 작성하는 데 두 시간이 걸렸다.

2 Add a spoonful of olive ____________ to the salad.
샐러드에 한 스푼 정도의 올리브 기름을 넣어 주세요.

3 What was the ____________ topic of the discussion?
그 토론의 주된 주제는 무엇이었습니까?

4 It is now a ____________ of time, not of money.
그것은 이제 돈이 아니라 시간의 문제다.

5 The boy is wearing a ____________ of an eagle.
그 소년은 독수리 가면을 쓰고 있었다.

G 그림과 낱말이 잘못 짝지어진 것을 고르세요. .... (　　　　　)

ⓐ  learn

ⓑ  people

ⓒ  angel

ⓓ  miss

H 낱말과 어울리는 그림을 연결하세요.

1 match •　　　　　　• ⓐ 

2 high •　　　　　　• ⓑ 

Study More

off의 여러 의미

- [부사] : 공간적,시간적으로 '멀리, 혹은 '멀리 떨어져'의 의미

  to run **off** 뛰어 달아나다　　to get **off** at the next bus stop 다음 정류장에서 내리다

- [형용사] : '작동을 멈춘', '꺼져 있는'

  The air conditioner is **off** now. 에어컨이 지금 꺼져있다.

Day 29

MP3

561 **bite** [bait]

동 물다 명 물기, 무는 것 bite-bit-bitten

bite into an apple 사과를 베어 물다 take a bite 한 입 베어 물다

562 **mountain** [máuntən]

명 산

climb a mountain 산을 오르다
the top of a mountain 산 정상

563 **comic** [kámik]

형 웃기는, 재미있는, 만화의

a comic story 웃기는 이야기 read comic books 만화책을 읽다

564 **large** [lɑːrdʒ]

형 큰, 거대한 large-larger-largest

a large table 큰 탁자
a large number of people 많은 수의 사람들

565 **size** [saiz]

명 크기

the same size 같은 크기 a small-size hat 작은 크기의 모자

566 **smell** [smel]

동 냄새를 맡다 명 냄새 smell-smelled-smelled

smell the flower 꽃 냄새를 맡다
a strong smell of garlic 마늘의 강한 냄새

567 **hear** [hiər]

동 듣다 hear-heard-heard

hear your voice 당신의 목소리를 듣다 hear well 잘 듣다

568 **try** [trai]

동 노력하다, ~해보다 try-tried-tried

try to+동사원형 ~을 시도하다, ~하려고 노력하다
try to remember 기억하려고 노력하다

569 **name** [neim]

명 이름

a family name 성씨
Write your name on the paper. 이름을 종이 위에 써라.

570 **elephant** [éləfənt]

명 코끼리

a herd of elephants 한 무리의 코끼리
the tusk of an elephant 코끼리의 상아

Daily Test

| 월 일 |

A 우리말에 맞게 빈 칸에 알맞은 단어를 쓰세요.

1 The dog __________ into an apple. 그 개는 사과를 베어 물었다.

2 His hobby is to climb __________. 그의 취미는 산을 오르는 것이다.

3 Robert read __________ books all day yesterday. Robert는 어제 하루 종일 만화책을 읽었다.

4 Linda came from a __________ family. Linda는 대가족 출신이다.

5 Your shirt and this shirt are the same __________. 당신의 셔츠와 이 셔츠는 같은 크기에요.

6 These chocolate cookies taste and __________ good. 이 초콜릿 쿠키들은 맛과 향이 좋다.

7 Didn't you __________ anything? 무슨 소리 나는 것 못 들었니?

8 The boy __________ to climb up the tree. 소년은 그 나무에 오르려고 애를 썼다.

9 Write your __________ and phone number. 당신의 이름과 전화 번호를 적으세요.

10 The __________ is the largest land animal in the world. 코끼리는 세계에서 제일 큰 육지동물이다.

B 빈 칸에 알맞은 단어를 고르세요.

1 He __________ to make new pants.
① tried ② milk ③ luck ④ start ⑤ nice

2 I took a large __________ of the pizza.
① nice ② pieces ③ ate ④ bite ⑤ neck

3 There is a strange __________ in the room.
① hear ② smell ③ kind ④ joke ⑤ size

Day 29

MP3

571 **fox** [fɑks]

명 여우

a wild and old fox 늙은 야생여우
The Fox and the Grapes 여우와 포도

572 **neck** [nek]

명 목, 목 부분

a short neck 짧은 목　　the neck of a bottle 병의 목부분

573 **milk** [milk]

명 우유

drink milk 우유를 마시다　　a bottle of milk 우유 한 병

574 **nest** [nest]

명 둥지

a bird nest 새 둥지　　build a nest 둥지를 만들다

575 **new** [nju:]

형 새로운

a new computer 새로운 컴퓨터　　the new year 신년

576 **nice** [nais]

형 좋은, 멋진　nice-nicer-nicest

nice weather 좋은 날씨　　a nice movie 멋진 영화

577 **now** [nau]

부 지금, 이제

right now 바로 지금　　from now on 지금부터

578 **meat** [mi:t]

명 고기

eat meat 고기를 먹다　　fresh meat 신선한 고기

579 **meet** [mi:t]

동 만나다　meet-met-met　　명 meeting 만남, 회의

Nice to meet you. 만나서 반갑습니다.
Meet me at the airport. 공항에서 만나자.

580 **luck** [lʌk]

명 운, 운수　　형 lucky 운이 좋은, 행운의

good luck 행운　　a lucky day 운이 좋은 날

Daily Test

| 월 일 |

A 우리말에 맞게 빈 칸에 알맞은 단어를 쓰세요.

1 A ______________ was walking through the forest. 여우는 숲 속을 걷고 있었다.

2 A giraffe has a long ______________. 기린은 긴 목을 가지고 있다.

3 I want to drink fresh ______________. 나는 신선한 우유를 마시고 싶다.

4 There is a bird ______________ in the tree. 나무 위에 새 둥지가 있다.

5 Tiffany bought a ______________ skirt. Tiffany는 새 스커트를 샀다.

6 The weather is ______________ today. 오늘은 날씨가 좋다.

7 Where are you going ______________? 지금 어디 가는 중이야?

8 Sarah doesn't eat ______________. Sarah는 고기를 먹지 않는다.

9 Should we ______________ at the park at seven? 7시에 공원에서 만날까?

10 I wish you good ______________. 당신의 행운을 빕니다.

B 빈 칸에 알맞은 단어를 고르세요.

1 Let me show you my ______________ computer.
① difficult ② nest ③ new ④ name ⑤ luck

2 I ______________ Helen at the concert hall.
① luck ② say ③ match ④ think ⑤ met

3 I was ______________ to find the book.
① comic ② lucky ③ large ④ bad ⑤ nest

Day 30

MP3

581 □ **iron** [aiərn]

명 철, 다리미

an iron gate 철문　　an ironing board 다리미 판

582 □ **share** [ʃɛər]

동 공유하다　share-shared-shared

share a room 방을 함께 쓰다
share information 정보를 공유하다

583 □ **terrible** [térəbl]

형 심각한　　유 horrific 끔찍한

a terrible accident 심각한 사고
a terrible nightmare 끔찍한 악몽

584 □ **real** [ríːəl]

형 실제의

in real life 실제 생활에서　　look real 실제처럼 보이다

585 □ **perfect** [pə́ːrfikt]

형 완벽한　　명 perfection 완벽, 완전

a perfect day 완벽한 하루　　a perfect score 완벽한 점수

586 □ **repeat** [ripíːt]

동 반복하다　repeat-repeated-repeated

repeat a mistake 실수를 반복하다
repeat a question 질문을 반복하다

587 □ **sink** [siŋk]

명 싱크대　동 가라앉다　sink-sank-sunk

a bathroom sink 욕실 싱크대
sink in the deep sea 깊은 바다로 가라앉다

588 □ **ant** [ænt]

명 개미

an ant's nest 개미집　　a red ant 불개미

589 □ **potato** [pətéitou]

명 감자　　복 potatoes

eat potatoes 감자를 먹다　　boil potatoes 감자를 삶다

590 □ **turtle** [tə́ːrtl]

명 거북이

a sea turtle 바다거북　　The Turtle Ship 거북선

Daily Test

| 월 일 |

A 우리말에 맞게 빈 칸에 알맞은 단어를 쓰세요.

1 Our new chair is made of ________________. 우리의 새 의자는 철로 만들어졌다.

2 We should ________________ this room for a week. 우리는 일주일동안 이 방을 같이 써야 한다.

3 I had a ________________ nightmare last night. 나는 지난 밤 끔찍한 악몽을 꿨다.

4 The bird in the picture looks ________________. 그림 속 새는 실제처럼 보인다.

5 It was a ________________ day. 완벽한 하루였다.

6 Thomas ________________ the question. Thomas는 질문을 반복했다.

7 The boat started to ________________ in the river. 그 배는 강으로 가라앉기 시작했다.

8 The boys are looking at ________________ marching in a line. 소년들이 개미가 줄을 지어 가는 것을 보고 있다.

9 Helen baked ________________ for the party. Helen은 파티를 위해 감자를 구웠다.

10 Sea ________________ usually lay around 100 eggs at a time. 바다거북은 보통 한 번에 100여 개의 알을 낳는다.

B 빈 칸에 알맞은 단어를 고르세요.

1 He had a ________________ accident last week.

① problem ② abroad ③ terrible ④ share ⑤ clear

2 I don't want to ________________ the same mistake.

① different ② trouble ③ perfect ④ repeat ⑤ sink

3 I ________________ my cake with friends.

① heard ② shared ③ sank ④ studied ⑤ place

Day 30

MP3

591 **professor** [prəfésər]
명 교수
a college professor 대학 교수
a biology professor 생물학 교수

592 **abroad** [əbrɔ́:d]
부 외국에
go abroad 외국에 가다　study abroad 해외 유학하다

593 **present** [prézənt]
명 선물, 현재
a Christmas present 크리스마스 선물　the present 현재

594 **kick** [kik]
동 차다　kick-kicked-kicked
kick a soccer ball 축구공을 차다　kick a goal 골을 차 넣다

595 **sell** [sel]
동 팔다　sell-sold-sold
sell a car 자동차를 팔다　sold out 다 팔린, 매진된

596 **toilet** [tɔ́ilit]
명 화장실
a public toilet 공중 화장실　go to the toilet 화장실에 가다

597 **sea** [si:]
명 바다
by the sea 바닷가에서　under the sea 바다 속에

598 **study** [stʌ́di]
명 공부　동 공부하다　study-studied-studied
study hard 열심히 공부하다　study math 수학을 공부하다

599 **garden** [gá:rdən]
명 정원
a back garden 뒤뜰　in the garden 정원에서

600 **place** [pleis]
명 장소
a picnic place 소풍 장소　a birthplace 출생지

Daily Test

| 월 일 |

A 우리말에 맞게 빈 칸에 알맞은 단어를 쓰세요.

1 Nick is a biology ______________ at university. Nick은 대학에서 생물학 교수로 있다.

2 Mina's family goes ______________ every winter. 매 겨울마다 미나의 가족은 외국에 간다.

3 Thank you for the great Christmas ______________. 멋진 크리스마스 선물 고맙습니다.

4 Yohan ______________ the ball. 요한은 공을 찼다.

5 I want to ______________ my old car. 나는 내 오래된 차를 팔고 싶다.

6 Who's in the ______________? 화장실에 누가 있니?

7 Wendy lived by the ______________. Wendy는 바닷가에서 살았다.

8 Ted is ______________ to be a science teacher. Ted는 과학선생님이 되기 위해 공부하고 있다.

9 Our ______________ is full of spring flowers. 우리 정원은 봄 꽃들로 가득 찼다.

10 Central Park is my mother's favorite ______________. Central Park는 엄마가 가장 좋아하는 장소이다

B 빈 칸에 알맞은 단어를 고르세요.

1 Julia ______________ abroad for five years.

① sank ② studied ③ shared ④ repeated ⑤ kicked

2 Does this store ______________ swim suits?

① sell ② sold ③ study ④ finish ⑤ sink

3 There is no ______________ like home.

① size ② abroad ③ toilet ④ ballon ⑤ place

Review Test 15

Day 29 + Day 30 | 월 일 |

A 우리말에 맞게 빈 칸에 알맞은 단어를 쓰세요.

1 ________________ well 잘 듣다

2 ________________ to remember 기억하려고 노력하다

3 ________________ weather 좋은 날씨

4 from ________________ on 지금부터

5 ________________ me at the airport 공항에서 만나자

6 ________________ information 정보를 공유하다

7 ________________ a question 질문을 반복하다

8 a biology ________________ 생물학 교수

9 the ________________ 현재

10 ________________ a car 자동차를 팔다

B 다음 영어 풀이에 알맞은 어휘를 〈보기〉에서 고르세요.

보기	size	sea	iron	mountain	elephant

1 ____________ : an area of land that rises higher than a hill

2 ____________ : how big or small a thing can be

3 ____________ : a large grey animal with a long and flexible nose

4 ____________ : a strong and hard metal used for cars, airplanes, and tools.

5 ____________ : a body salt water covered in whole or in part by land

C 다음 단어의 관계가 A:B=C:D가 되도록 알맞은 단어를 골라 빈 칸에 적으세요.

1 ______________ : apple = buy : bread

① red ② make ③ bite
④ round ⑤ delicious

2 climb : ______________ = clean : room

① mountain ② cleaned ③ bag
④ milk ⑤ sing

3 ______________ : nose = hear : ear

① see ② eyes ③ smelled
④ smell ⑤ listen

4 study : ______________ = work : hard

① book ② abroad ③ English
④ studied ⑤ math

5 ______________ : accident = real : diamond

① car ② share ③ His
④ easy ⑤ terrible

D 문맥에 맞게 다음 문장을 완성하세요.

1 Write your name •	• a	full of spring flowers.
2 Our new chair •	• b	and phone number.
3 I wish you •	• c	good luck.
4 The bird in the picture •	• d	looks real.
5 Our garden is •	• e	is made of iron.

E 문장을 읽고 문맥에 적절한 단어를 고르세요.

1 He was so thirsty that he drank up the (large/comic) bottle of water.

2 Jinsu (studied/kicked) the ball into the goal and scored a point.

3 The bookstore is our favorite meeting (place/abroad).

4 Bill wants to write (comic/terrible) stories to make people smile.

5 It is the (perfect/large) weather to go to the beach.

F 문장의 빈칸에 알맞은 단어를 〈보기〉에서 찾아 쓰세요. (필요하면 형태를 고치세요.)

보기	fox	neck	milk	turtle	potato

1 The little girl held her father around his ____________ for joy.
소녀는 기뻐서 아버지의 목을 감싸 안았다.

2 He raises cows to get ____________.
그는 우유를 얻기 위해서 소를 키운다.

3 Mother cut the ____________ in half and baked them in the oven.
어머니는 감자를 반으로 잘라서 오븐에 구웠다.

4 It was interesting to see living ____________ in the aquarium.
수족관에서 살아있는 거북을 본 것은 아주 흥미로웠다.

5 ____________ use their tails to keep them warm in cold weather.
여우들은 추운 날씨에 몸을 따뜻하게 유지하기 위해 꼬리를 사용한다.

G 그림에 해당하는 낱말을 〈보기〉에서 골라 쓰세요.

1

(   )

2

(   )

3

(   )

4

(   )

5

(   )

6

(   )

보기 nest toilet study new sink present

Study More

동사 try의 용법

- [try to+동사] : '~을 해보다/시도하다'
  He **tried to** solve the question by himself. 그는 그 문제를 혼자 풀려고 해보았다.
- [try on something] [try something on] : '(옷/신발 등) 입어/신어 보다'
  Can I just **try on** these pants? 이 바지 한 번 입어볼 수 있을까요?

Index

Answer Key

정답 및 해설

Answer Key

Day 01

Daily Test 1 P. 09

A
1 acts
2 actor
3 alone
4 always
5 teaches
6 burning
7 green
8 blue
9 sky
10 astronaut

B
1 ① teach
2 ② alone
3 ⑤ burnt

Daily Test 2 P. 11

A
1 space
2 album
3 grapes
4 apple
5 able
6 about
7 above
8 stomachache
9 across
10 ambulance

B
1 ③ able
2 ① above
3 ⑤ across

Day 02

Daily Test 1 P. 13

A
1 clothes
2 jeans
3 animals
4 cow
5 clean
6 dirty
7 cheap
8 expensive
9 drying
10 wet

B
1 ② expensive
2 ① clean
3 ⑤ cheap

Daily Test 2 P. 15

A
1 character
2 drew
3 breakfast
4 eat
5 boiled
6 borrow
7 book
8 inside
9 outside
10 angry

B
1 ① boiled
2 ⑤ borrow
3 ① inside

Review Test 01

Day 01 + Day 02 P. 16

A
1 always
2 breakfast
3 able
4 about
5 across
6 clean
7 dirty
8 boil
9 inside
10 angry

B
1 ache
2 dry
3 boil
4 cheap
5 ambulance

C
1 ③ animal
2 ① alone
3 ⑤ cartoon
4 ② apple
5 ④ outside

D
1 a
2 c
3 e
4 b
5 d

E
1 drew
2 ambulance

3 actor
4 drying
5 eats

해석

1. 민수는 쥐와 고양이에 대한 만화를 그렸다.
2. 구급차는 우리 엄마를 병원으로 옮겼다.
3. Tim은 액션 영화 배우가 되고 싶어한다.
4. 유나는 그녀의 머리를 수건으로 말리는 중이다.
5. 지민은 그녀가 일어나자마자 아침을 먹는다.

F

1 teaches
2 cheap
3 sky
4 jeans
5 space

G

1 ache
2 act
3 astronaut
4 boil
5 eat
6 wet

Day 03

Daily Test 1 P. 21

A

1 club
2 join
3 called
4 phone
5 easy
6 difficult
7 morning
8 night
9 end
10 began

B

1 ① join
2 ④ difficult
3 ⑤ begin

Daily Test 2 P. 23

A

1 happy
2 bird
3 rabbit
4 noodle
5 address
6 afford
7 afraid
8 again
9 age
10 ankle

B

1 ① afraid
2 ③ age
3 ② address

Day 04

Daily Test 1 P. 25

A

1 left
2 radio
3 big
4 salt
5 Listen
6 math
7 make
8 cake
9 kite
10 flew

B

1 ② big
2 ③ make
3 ① listening

Daily Test 2 P. 27

A

1 guitar
2 room
3 invented
4 right
5 small
6 music
7 ago
8 ahead
9 almost
10 already

B

1 ① invented
2 ② small
3 ④ ahead

Review Test 02

Day 03 + Day 04 P. 28

A

1 call
2 end
3 address
4 afford
5 afraid
6 night

7 make
8 ago
9 ahead
10 almost

B
1 club
2 radio
3 bird
4 invent
5 kite

C
1 ③ join
2 ② morning
3 ⑤ invent
4 ① begin
5 ④ room

D
1 a
2 c
3 e
4 b
5 d

E
1 radio
2 club
3 age
4 big
5 fly

해석

1. 네가 자러 갈 때 라디오를 끄는 걸 잊지 마렴.
2. Joe는 독서 동아리에 일원이 되길 원한다.
3. 16살의 나이에, 그는 유명한 테니스 선수가 되었다.
4. 그의 손은 매우 커서 그가 한 손으로 농구공을 집을 수 있었다.
5. 그 마을 대부분에 아이들은 연을 날리러 갔다.

F
1 rabbit
2 birds
3 small
4 ankle
5 noodle

G
ⓐ ankle

H
1 ⓐ
2 ⓑ

Day 05

Daily Test 1 P. 33

A
1 before
2 boring
3 safe
4 area
5 food
6 body
7 leg
8 sunny
9 away
10 baby

B
1 ⑤ areas
2 ③ away
3 ④ boring

Daily Test 2 P. 35

A
1 dish
2 band
3 movie
4 foot
5 dangerous
6 autumn
7 sunglasses
8 delicious
9 bamboo
10 after

B
1 ① after
2 ③ dangerous
3 ⑤ delicious

Day 06

Daily Test 1 P. 37

A
1 save
2 money
3 brushes
4 necklace
5 bark
6 coat
7 jacket
8 seafood
9 pretty
10 got

B
1 ② get
2 ① saved
3 ④ brush

Daily Test 2 P. 39

A
1 lost
2 smart
3 doctor
4 chose
5 dentist
6 bar
7 barber
8 ring
9 basket
10 bath

B
1 ③ smart
2 ① chose
3 ④ bath

Review Test 03

Day 05 + Day 06 P. 40

A
1 area
2 away
3 food
4 foot
5 dangerous
6 save
7 bark
8 get
9 lose
10 choose

B
1 boring
2 dangerous
3 bath
4 sun
5 delicious

C
1 ① safe
2 ② brush
3 ⑤ seafood
4 ③ sunglasses
5 ① necklace

D
1 c
2 b
3 e
4 d
5 a

E
1 jacket
2 money
3 barber
4 dentist
5 after

해석
1. 밖이 매우 춥구나. 나갈 때 겉옷을 입도록 해.
2. 그는 새 컴퓨터를 살 만큼 충분한 돈이 없었다.
3. Ted는 머리를 자르러 이발소에 갈 예정이다.
4. 유미는 충치가 생겨서 치과에 갈 예정이다.
5. 하늘은 비가 멈춘 뒤 맑아졌다.

F
1 pretty
2 body
3 dish
4 bamboo
5 smart

G
1 boring
2 delicious
3 broken
4 basket
5 doctor
6 ring

Day 07

Daily Test 1 P. 45

A
1 day
2 become
3 minutes
4 month
5 King
6 pull
7 soldier
8 princess
9 pushed
10 beans

B
1 ② pushed
2 ② minutes
3 ① became

Daily Test 2 P. 47

A
1 different
2 subject
3 science
4 flowers
5 prince
6 same
7 crown
8 beat
9 Because
10 hours

B

1 ⑤ different
2 ④ same
3 ① because

Day 08

Daily Test 1 P. 49

A

1 fixed
2 useful
3 box
4 hobby
5 fresh
6 air
7 open
8 cloudy
9 Purple
10 vegetable

B

1 ④ fixed
2 ④ useful
3 ① opened

Daily Test 2 P. 51

A

1 use
2 favorite
3 helped
4 bed
5 bell
6 between
7 notice board
8 boat
9 bones
10 ride

B

1 ① helped
2 ④ favorite
3 ② between

Review Test 04

Day 07 + Day 08 P. 52

A

1 become
2 month
3 different
4 same
5 Because
6 fix
7 useful
8 vegetables
9 between
10 beans

B

1 pull
2 beat
3 ride
4 fresh
5 push

C

1 ① cloudy
2 ③ help
3 ⑤ open
4 ② subject
5 ④ princess

D

1 b
2 d
3 c
4 a
5 e

E

1 open
2 bed
3 box
4 Use
5 air

해석

1. 오늘은 매우 덥구나. Becky. 창문 좀 열어 주겠니?
2. 그녀는 매우 피곤해서 빨리 자러 갔어요.
3. 그 낡은 책들을 여기 플라스틱 상자 안에 넣어주세요.
4. 만약 네가 중국어를 공부하기 원한다면 이 사전을 이용하렴.
5. 그는 공을 그가 할 수 있는 만큼 높이 공기 중으로 던졌다.

F

1 beat
2 favorite
3 bean
4 hobby
5 doorbell

G

ⓐ fresh

F

1 ⓑ
2 ⓐ

Day 09

Daily Test 1 P. 57

A

1 art
2 wrote
3 bought
4 brain
5 sing

6 plays
7 broken
8 planting
9 bridge
10 sorry

B
1 ① played
2 ② plants
3 ④ bought

Daily Test 2 P. 59

A
1 future
2 washed
3 queen
4 Christmas card
5 tickets
6 brand
7 game
8 breathe
9 Thank
10 artist

B
1 ① future
2 ② Thank
3 ⑤ breathe

Day 10

Daily Test 1 P. 61

A
1 watches
2 visited
3 grandparents
4 hungry
5 full
6 thick
7 thin
8 family
9 cousin
10 Mix

B
1 ⑤ visiting
2 ③ thick
3 ④ watched

Daily Test 2 P. 63

A
1 seasons
2 fall
3 sports
4 football
5 carrying
6 nurse
7 camera
8 dead
9 business
10 butter

B
1 ① carry
2 ① season
3 ④ business

Review Test 05

Day 09 + Day 10 P. 64

A
1 sing
2 future
3 break
4 football
5 breathe
6 watch
7 queen
8 mix
9 fall
10 carry

B
1 breathe
2 nurse
3 queen
4 bridge
5 plant

C
1 ① artist
2 ④ buy
3 ② season
4 ⑤ full
5 ② wash

D
1 e
2 c
3 b
4 a
5 d

E
1 butter
2 hungry
3 camera
4 dead
5 thin

해석

1. 이 빵은 위에 버터를 바르면 맛이 더 좋아져요.
2. 나는 정말 배고파. 뭐라도 좀 먹어야겠어.
3. 저는 봄 꽃의 사진을 찍기 위해서 저만의 카메라가 필요해요.
4. 만약 네가 꽃에게 물을 주지 않는다면, 그들은 곧 죽을 거야.
5. 이 책은 얇지만 이해 하는 데 시간이 걸릴 거에요.

F

1 visited
2 tickets
3 nurse
4 grandparents
5 art

G

1 brain
2 bridge
3 write
4 family
5 thick
6 dead

Day 11

Daily Test 1 P. 69

A

1 plane
2 slowly
3 strong
4 weak
5 go
6 pilot
7 chance
8 baked
9 congratulate
10 faster

B

1 ② weak
2 ① congratulated
3 ② baking

Daily Test 2 P. 71

A

1 warm
2 Stretch
3 Bye
4 cared
5 center
6 Bring
7 church
8 check
9 stopped
10 cartoon

B

1 ① bring
2 ③ stopped
3 ④ cartoon

Day 12

Daily Test 1 P. 73

A

1 date
2 drive
3 brave
4 brown
5 aunt
6 butterfly
7 chewing
8 introduce
9 jump
10 off

B

1 ③ drive
2 ④ off
3 ① introduce

Daily Test 2 P. 75

A

1 homework
2 surfed
3 enjoyed
4 party
5 corner
6 curly
7 curtains
8 bright
9 deep
10 scary

B

1 ② bright
2 ④ enjoys
3 ⑤ deep

Review Test 06

Day 11 + Day 12 P. 76

A

1 weak
2 chance
3 congratulate
4 center
5 check
6 bright
7 chew
8 enjoy
9 date
10 deep

B

1 stretch
2 pilot
3 bake
4 aunt
5 party

C

1 ① scary
2 ③ introduce
3 ① brought

4 ⑤ surf
5 ④ butterfly

D
1 a
2 d
3 b
4 e
5 c

E
1 caring
2 goes
3 stopped
4 close
5 party

해석
1. Lucy는 어린 고양이를 돌보는 중이다.
2. 우리 아빠는 차로 출근 하십니다.
3. 그 늙은 여인은 도움을 청하기 위해 소년을 멈춰 세웠다.
4. Brian, 나는 지금 자야 해. 커튼 좀 쳐 주겠니?
5. 우리는 Tim이 다른 학교로 전학 가기 때문에 송별회를 열 예정이다.

F
1 warm
2 strong
3 corner
4 brown
5 scary

G
ⓓ drive

H
1 ⓐ
2 ⓑ

Day 13

Daily Test 1 P. 81

A
1 country
2 dolls
3 busy
4 free
5 early
6 late
7 round
8 lives
9 back
10 ball

B
1 ① free
2 ③ back
3 ① busy

Daily Test 2 P. 83

A
1 circle
2 ready
3 newspaper
4 read
5 whole
6 noon
7 wish
8 world
9 worry
10 together

B
1 ⑤ together
2 ③ ready
3 ④ worry

Day 14

Daily Test 1 P. 85

A
1 poor
2 sweet
3 laugh
4 Ducks
5 candies
6 spicy
7 looked
8 fan
9 upset
10 won

B
1 ③ poor
2 ② win
3 ④ sweet

Daily Test 2 P. 87

A
1 pay
2 child
3 tooth
4 dropped
5 factory
6 rich
7 Excuse
8 errand
9 famous
10 behind

B
1 ③ famous
2 ① paid
3 ① Excuse

Review Test 07

Day 13 + Day 14 P. 88

A
1 busy
2 late
3 read
4 whole
5 noon
6 poor
7 laugh
8 upset
9 excuse
10 behind

B
1 country
2 doll
3 newspaper
4 fan
5 child

C
1 ① country
2 ④ free
3 ③ rich
4 ⑤ paid
5 ② tooth

D
1 d
2 b
3 a
4 e
5 c

E
1 lives
2 together
3 Ducks
4 dropping
5 famous

해석

1. 그는 그의 부모님과 멀리 떨어져 산다.
2. 많은 사람들이 쓰러진 나무를 함께 옮기기 위해서 모였다.
3. 오리와 백조는 같은 새 과에 속한다.
4. 어린 소년은 재미로 엄마의 동전을 떨어뜨리는 중이다.
5. 그 축구 선수는 그의 독특한 공을 차는 방식으로 유명하다.

F
1 early
2 circle
3 spicy
4 errand
5 round

G
1 back
2 newspaper
3 wish
4 worry
5 look
6 win

Day 15

Daily Test 1 P. 93

A
1 red
2 Blood
3 blocks
4 things
5 monkeys
6 train
7 contest
8 keeps
9 secret
10 bad

B
1 ③ contest
2 ① kept
3 ② secret

Daily Test 2 P. 95

A
1 near
2 earth
3 tradition
4 yet
5 textbook
6 theater
7 then
8 pieces
9 throat
10 tomorrow

B
1 ④ tomorrow
2 ④ yet
3 ① nearest

Day 16

Daily Test 1 P. 97

A
1 work
2 rest
3 park
4 swimming
5 beach
6 oven
7 restaurant
8 president
9 student
10 designed

B

1 ③ work
2 ④ designed
3 ③ beach

Daily Test 2 P. 99

A

1 moon
2 office
3 often
4 pool
5 only
6 orange
7 meal
8 seat
9 parade
10 awake

B

1 ③ meal
2 ② often
3 ② only

Review Test 08

Day 15 + Day 16 P. 100

A

1 contest
2 Keep
3 tradition
4 yet
5 then
6 work
7 design
8 only
9 meal
10 awake

B

1 throat
2 park
3 oven
4 seat
5 contest

C

1 ② moon
2 ④ piece
3 ① secret
4 ② near
5 ⑤ beach

D

1 d
2 a
3 b
4 e
5 c

E

1 bad
2 throat
3 swim
4 restaurant
5 often

해석

1. 그녀는 그 나쁜 소식을 들은 뒤 울기 시작했다.
2. 그는 기침을 많이 했고 목이 아팠다.
3. 바다에서 혼자 수영하는 것은 위험하다.
4. 우리는 엄마의 생신에 좋은 이탈리아 식당에 가서 저녁을 먹었다.
5. 그녀는 새 책을 읽기 위해 종종 도서관에 간다.

F

1 office
2 monkeys
3 textbooks
4 tomorrow
5 pool

G

ⓒ theater

H

1 ⓑ
2 ⓐ

Day 17

Daily Test 1 P. 105

A

1 top
2 see
3 blind
4 police
5 fire
6 painting
7 wall
8 rock
9 stick
10 treated

B

1 ③ blind
2 ① treated
3 ② painting

Daily Test 2 P. 107

A

1 airport
2 Museum
3 sick
4 Everything
5 tonight
6 touch
7 towel
8 tower
9 ship
10 shoulder

B
1 ① sick
2 ② touched
3 ⑤ ship

Day 18

Daily Test 1 P. 109

A
1 heavy
2 closet
3 snack
4 window
5 ask
6 price
7 problem
8 drink
9 once
10 peaches

B
1 ① heavy
2 ⑤ price
3 ② problem

Daily Test 2 P. 111

A
1 second
2 grew
3 goats
4 house
5 twice
6 pea
7 peace
8 first
9 smiles
10 wide

B
1 ② second
2 ③ grew
3 ② wider

Review Test 09

Day 17 + Day 18 P. 112

A
1 twice
2 wall
3 treat
4 airport
5 ship
6 peas
7 ask
8 once
9 second
10 first

B
1 closet
2 snack
3 museum
4 tower
5 top

C
1 ① blind
2 ③ top
3 ⑤ problem
4 ② goat
5 ④ house

D
1 a
2 c
3 d
4 b
5 e

E
1 touch
2 window
3 price
4 smiles
5 fire

해석
1. 너는 그 개를 만져서는 안 돼. 그것이 널 물 거야.
2. 난 상쾌한 공기가 필요해요. 창문 좀 열어줄래요?
3. 나는 네가 그 가게에서 더 싼 값에 그 자전거를 살 수 있었다고 생각해.
4. 나는 그녀가 나를 향해 웃을 때 행복하다.
5. 큰 불이 산의 대부분을 태웠다.

F
1 rock
2 peach
3 peace
4 police
5 drink

G
1 paint
2 shoulder
3 sick
4 towel
5 closet
6 heavy

Day 19

Daily Test 1 P. 117

A
1 wears
2 shirt
3 caught
4 pocket
5 City

6 power
7 sits
8 week
9 usually
10 map

B
1 ① wears
2 ② Sit
3 ② caught

Daily Test 2 P. 119

A
1 exercise
2 gym
3 pumpkin
4 library
5 words
6 dictionary
7 sometimes
8 soap
9 Guide
10 feel

B
1 ① guide
2 ④ felt
3 ② sometimes

Day 20

Daily Test 1 P. 121

A
1 horse
2 race
3 shoes
4 feed
5 holiday
6 town
7 afternoon
8 fever
9 cough
10 windy

B
1 ① race
2 ③ holiday
3 ② feed

Daily Test 2 P. 123

A
1 young
2 old
3 straight
4 Bend
5 store
6 moment
7 notebooks
8 energy
9 festival
10 fighting

B
1 ① fought
2 ② young
3 ② Bend

Review Test 10

Day 19 + Day 20 P. 124

A
1 wear
2 power
3 guide
4 dictionary
5 sometimes
6 holiday
7 fever
8 feed
9 moment
10 word

B
1 map
2 gym
3 race
4 word
5 moment

C
1 ③ map
2 ① city
3 ④ bent
4 ② exercise
5 ⑤ energy

D
1 e
2 a
3 b
4 d
5 c

E
1 shirt
2 straight
3 sit
4 gym
5 shoes

해석

1. 너는 이미 젖었구나. 당장 네 셔츠를 갈아 입으렴!
2. 이 길 끝까지 쭉 직진하세요.
3. 의자를 가져와서 앉으세요.
4. 그는 약간의 운동을 하기 위해 매일 체육관에 간다.
5. 준기는 그의 아빠와 달리기 위해 런닝화를 샀다.

F
1 usually
2 notebook
3 soap
4 pocket
5 town

G
ⓒ run

H
1 ⓐ
2 ⓑ

Day 21

Daily Test 1 P. 129

A
1 farm
2 hospital
3 follow
4 added
5 need
6 medicine
7 mirror
8 goal
9 threw
10 forest

B
1 ② hospital
2 ④ throw
3 ① Follow

Daily Test 2 P. 131

A
1 bread
2 pillow
3 station
4 pear
5 pencil
6 find
7 flag
8 flu
9 invite
10 turn

B
1 ① turned
2 ⑤ found
3 ③ invited

Day 22

Daily Test 1 P. 133

A
1 took
2 picture
3 pass
4 practiced
5 travel
6 bee
7 honey
8 lovely
9 bank
10 Pig

B
1 ① took
2 ④ practices
3 ③ travel

Daily Test 2 P. 135

A
1 post office
2 runny
3 quiz
4 history
5 fork
6 from
7 fun
8 speak
9 gift
10 gave

B
1 ⑤ from
2 ② history
3 ③ speak

Review Test 11

Day 21 + Day 22 P. 136

A
1 invite
2 mirror
3 goal
4 pillow
5 find
6 take
7 practice
8 post office
9 runny
10 from

B
1 farm
2 pencil
3 quiz
4 fork
5 forest

C
1 ① lovely
2 ③ speak

3 ② quiz
4 ③ gave
5 ⑤ farm

D
1 b
2 a
3 d
4 c
5 e

E
1 bread
2 flu
3 need
4 add
5 turn

해석
1. 엄마는 집에서 빵을 굽는 걸 좋아하신다.
2. Amy는 독감 주사를 맞기 위해 병원에 갔다.
3. 나는 이 상자들을 옮기는 데 당신의 도움이 필요해요.
4. 그 수프는 너무 짜요. 물을 좀 더 넣는 게 어때요?
5. 이 앞 길은 막혔어요. 우리는 왼쪽으로 돌아가야 해요.

F
1 pear
2 travel
3 picture
4 history
5 Pigs

G
1 flag
2 hospital
3 medicine
4 throw
5 honey
6 pass

Day 23

Daily Test 1 P. 141

A
1 pair
2 bottle
3 stove
4 magic
5 tall
6 pink
7 building
8 daughters
9 son
10 brother

B
1 ① bottle
2 ⑤ bought
3 ② daughter

Daily Test 2 P. 143

A
1 had
2 glue
3 grade
4 grammar
5 habit
6 hall
7 hamburger
8 happened
9 hat
10 sister

B
1 ② have
2 ④ grade
3 ⑤ happened

Day 24

Daily Test 1 P. 145

A
1 interesting
2 like
3 over
4 vacation
5 baseball
6 basketball
7 year
8 trip
9 wise
10 pets

B
1 ④ interesting
2 ③ vacation
3 ⑤ trip

Daily Test 2 P. 147

A
1 Pick
2 program
3 Put
4 subway
5 sure
6 surprised
7 sounds
8 health
9 Hens
10 here

B
1 ⑤ Put
2 ② sure
3 ① sounded

Review Test 12

Day 23 + Day 24 P. 148

A
1 year
2 daughter
3 habit
4 happened
5 have
6 interesting
7 baseball
8 trip
9 sound
10 here

B
1 stove
2 hall
3 hamburger
4 pet
5 hen

C
1 ② wisest
2 ④ pair
3 ③ building
4 ⑤ magician
5 ① pet

D
1 e
2 c
3 a
4 d
5 b

E
1 glue
2 hat
3 over
4 put
5 surprised

해석
1. 나는 엽서 위에 풀로 우표를 고정시켰다.
2. 그 남자는 그의 모자를 벗어서 관중들을 맞이했다.
3. 말은 울타리를 뛰어 넘어 도망갔다.
4. 그는 나오기 전에 부엌 탁자에 메모를 남겨 두었다.
5. 모두가 지난 밤 그 소식을 듣고 놀랐다.

F
1 health
2 tallest
3 grade
4 pink
5 pick

G
ⓑ grade

H
1 ⓐ
2 ⓑ

Day 25

Daily Test 1 P. 153

A
1 kinds
2 great
3 little
4 lesson
5 plastic
6 shop
7 social
8 hope
9 cut
10 onion

B
1 ② Cut
2 ① lessons
3 ② social

Daily Test 2 P. 155

A
1 mail
2 sent
3 hiking
4 hit
5 holding
6 hometown
7 hundreds
8 hurt
9 husband
10 idea

B
1 ① hometown
2 ③ hurt
3 ② held

Day 26

Daily Test 1 P. 157

A
1 life
2 sheep
3 mistake
4 street
5 camel
6 lake
7 blowing
8 balloon
9 answer
10 kid

B

1 ③ mistake
2 ④ answer
3 ② blew

Daily Test 2 P. 159

A

1 come
2 print
3 Island
4 joke
5 just
6 question
7 knee
8 knit
9 know
10 lady

B

1 ① comes
2 ④ question
3 ⑤ know

Review Test 13

Day 25 + Day 26 P. 160

A

1 kind
2 lessons
3 mail
4 life
5 idea
6 mistake
7 blow
8 camel
9 knit
10 know

B

1 plastic
2 shop
3 hike
4 hit
5 island

C

1 ① question
2 ⑤ less
3 ③ send
4 ④ came
5 ② society

D

1 a
2 c
3 d
4 e
5 b

E

1 hurt
2 hiking
3 printed
4 plastic
5 joke

해석

1. Jerry는 그가 어제 다리를 다쳤기 때문에 지금 걸을 수 없어요.
2. 경민은 산으로 도보여행 가는 것을 좋아한다.
3. 그녀는 선생님을 위해 그녀의 에세이를 한 부 인쇄했다.
4. 이 컵들은 플라스틱으로 만들어 졌다.
5. Derek의 농담은 교실에 있는 모든 사람들을 웃게 했다.

F

1 sheep
2 onion
3 hometown
4 husband
5 leader

G

1 hit
2 hold
3 hope
4 answer
5 knee
6 lady

Day 27

Daily Test 1 P. 165

A

1 count
2 number
3 tasted
4 missed
5 member
6 glad
7 weigh
8 served
9 yesterday
10 high

B

1 ① counted
2 ② tastes
3 ④ weighs

Daily Test 2 P. 167

A

1 people
2 oil
3 later
4 spell
5 learn

6 leave
7 magazine
8 main
9 Many
10 market

B
1 ① learn
2 ⑤ left
3 ② many

Day 28

Daily Test 1 P. 169

A
1 think
2 Cover
3 Each
4 all
5 started
6 finish
7 angel
8 hurried
9 said
10 simple

B
1 ③ started
2 ⑤ thought
3 ② simple

Daily Test 2 P. 171

A
1 weekend
2 Welcome
3 every
4 letter
5 hill
6 marry
7 mask
8 match
9 matter
10 May

B
1 ③ welcomed
2 ② married
3 ⑤ matter

Review Test 14

Day 27 + Day 28 P. 172

A
1 count
2 miss
3 weigh
4 learn
5 glad
6 each
7 hurry
8 welcome
9 marry
10 off

B
1 number
2 weekend
3 letter
4 magazine
5 every

C
1 ① yesterday
2 ⑤ think
3 ② finish
4 ④ taste
5 ③ magazine

D
1 e
2 c
3 b
4 a
5 d

E
1 May
2 later
3 number
4 covered
5 glad

해석
1. 부탁을 해도 될까요?
2. 난 그것에 대해 얘기하기는 좀 이른 거 같다고 생각해. 우리 다음에 얘기하자.
3. 그는 그의 여동생에게 전화하고 싶었지만 그녀의 전화번호를 잊었다.
4. 산 전체가 지금 눈으로 뒤덮였다.
5. 그녀는 다시 집에 돌아와 그녀의 가족과 살게 되어 기뻤다.

F
1 simple
2 oil
3 main
4 matter
5 mask

G
ⓓ miss

H
1 ⓑ
2 ⓐ

Day 29

Daily Test 1 P. 177

A
1 bit
2 mountains
3 comic
4 large
5 size
6 smell
7 hear
8 tried
9 name
10 elephant

B
1 ① tried
2 ④ bite
3 ② smell

Daily Test 2 P. 179

A
1 fox
2 neck
3 milk
4 nest
5 new
6 nice
7 now
8 meat
9 meet
10 luck

B
1 ③ new
2 ⑤ met
3 ② lucky

Day 30

Daily Test 1 P. 181

A
1 iron
2 share
3 terrible
4 real
5 perfect
6 repeated
7 sink
8 ants
9 potatoes
10 turtles

B
1 ③ terrible
2 ④ repeat
3 ② shared

Daily Test 2 P. 183

A
1 professor
2 abroad
3 present
4 kicked
5 sell
6 toilet
7 sea
8 studying
9 garden
10 place

B
1 ② studied
2 ① sell
3 ⑤ place

Review Test 15

Day 29 + Day 30 P. 184

A
1 hear
2 try
3 nice
4 now
5 meet
6 share
7 repeat
8 professor
9 present
10 sell

B
1 mountain
2 size
3 elephant
4 iron
5 sea

C
1 ③ bite
2 ① mountain
3 ④ smell
4 ② abroad
5 ⑤ terrible

D
1 b
2 e
3 c
4 d
5 a

E
1 large
2 kicked
3 place

4 comic

5 perfect

해석

1. 그는 너무 목이 말라서 큰 물 한 병을 다 마셨다.
2. 진수는 골대로 공을 찼고 득점했다.
3. 그 서점은 우리가 가장 좋아하는 만남 장소에요.
4. Bill은 사람들을 웃게 만드는 재미 있는 이야기를 쓰고 싶어한다.
5. 해변에 가기 완벽한 날씨에요.

F

1 neck

2 milk

3 potatoes

4 turtles

5 Foxes

G

1 nest

2 new

3 present

4 sink

5 study

6 toilet

memo

memo

memo

memo

WORD MAX 1 5300

Workbook

WorldCom Edu

Workbook

WORD MAX 1 5300

WorldCom Edu

Workbook

Day 01

| 월 일 |

영어 단어에 해당하는 한국어 뜻을 함께 적으세요.

act	행동하다, 연기하다	act	행동하다, 연기하다
actor	남자 배우		
alone	홀로		
always	항상		
teach	가르치다		
burn	타다		
green	녹색; 녹색의, 초록빛의		
blue	파란색; 파란, 푸른		
sky	하늘		
astronaut	우주비행사		
space	우주		
album	앨범		
grape	포도		
apple	사과		
able	~할 수 있는		
about	~에 관해서		
above	~의 위에		
ache	아픔; 아프다, 쑤시다		
across	~을 가로질러		
ambulance	구급차		

다음 단어에 해당하는 영어 단어 또는 우리말을 쓰세요.

○___개 ×___개

영어	한국어
able	
about	
above	
ache	
across	
act	
actor	
album	
alone	
always	
ambulance	
apple	
astronaut	
blue	
burn	
grape	
green	
sky	
space	
teach	

한국어	영어
명 녹색 형 녹색의, 초록빛의	
전 ~에 관해서	
명 우주비행사	
동 가르치다	
명 남자 배우	
명 우주	
전 ~의 위에	
명 하늘	
명 사과	
동 타다	
명 포도	
형 ~할 수 있는	
명 아픔 동 아프다, 쑤시다	
전 ~을 가로질러	
부 항상	
부 홀로	
명 구급차	
명 앨범	
명 파란색 형 파란, 푸른	
동 행동하다, 연기하다	

Day 02

| 월 일 |

영어 단어에 해당하는 한국어 뜻을 함께 적으세요.

clothes	옷	clothes	옷
jeans	청바지		
animal	동물		
cow	소		
clean	깨끗한; 청소하다		
dirty	더러운		
cheap	값이 싼		
expensive	비싼		
dry	마른, 건조한; 말리다		
wet	젖은		
character	인물, 성격		
draw	그리다		
breakfast	아침 식사		
eat	먹다		
boil	끓이다		
borrow	빌리다		
book	책		
inside	내부; 안쪽에		
outside	겉, 바깥쪽; 외부의		
angry	화가 난		

다음 단어에 해당하는 영어 단어 또는 우리말을 쓰세요.

○____개 ×____개

영어	한국어
angry	
animal	
boil	
book	
borrow	
breakfast	
character	
cheap	
clean	
clothes	
cow	
dirty	
draw	
dry	
eat	
expensive	
inside	
jeans	
outside	
wet	

한국어	영어
형 마른, 건조한 동 말리다	
형 더러운	
동 먹다	
형 외부의	
동 그리다	
동 끓이다	
형 화가 난	
명 내부 전 안쪽에	
형 값이 싼	
명 소	
명 동물	
형 젖은	
명 옷	
형 깨끗한 동 청소하다	
동 빌리다	
명 인물, 성격	
명 아침 식사	
명 청바지	
형 비싼	
명 책	

Workbook

Day 03

| 월 일 |

영어 단어에 해당하는 한국어 뜻을 함께 적으세요.

club	동아리, 동호회	club	동아리, 동호회
join	가입하다		
call	부르다, 전화하다		
phone	전화		
easy	쉬운		
difficult	어려운		
morning	아침		
night	밤		
end	끝; 끝나다		
begin	시작하다		
happy	행복한		
bird	새		
rabbit	토끼		
noodle	국수		
address	주소		
afford	여유가 있다		
afraid	두려운		
again	다시		
age	나이		
ankle	발목		

다음 단어에 해당하는 영어 단어 또는 우리말을 쓰세요. ○____개 ×____개

영어	한국어
address	
afford	
afraid	
again	
age	
ankle	
begin	
bird	
call	
club	
difficult	
easy	
end	
happy	
join	
morning	
night	
noodle	
phone	
rabbit	

한국어	영어
동 가입하다	
형 어려운	
명 끝 동 끝나다	
동 여유가 있다	
명 국수	
명 나이	
형 쉬운	
명 동아리, 동호회	
명 밤	
동 부르다, 전화하다	
명 토끼	
동 시작하다	
형 행복한	
명 주소	
부 다시	
형 두려운	
명 전화	
명 발목	
명 새	
명 아침	

Workbook

Day 04

| 월 일 |

영어 단어에 해당하는 한국어 뜻을 함께 적으세요.

left	왼쪽의; 왼쪽에, 왼쪽으로	left	왼쪽의; 왼쪽에, 왼쪽으로
radio	라디오		
big	큰		
salt	소금		
listen	듣다		
math	수학		
make	만들다		
cake	케이크		
kite	연		
fly	날다, 날리다		
guitar	기타		
room	방		
invent	발명하다		
right	오른쪽의; 오른쪽으로, 우측으로		
small	작은		
music	음악		
ago	~전에		
ahead	앞으로, 앞에		
almost	거의		
already	이미		

다음 단어에 해당하는 영어 단어 또는 우리말을 쓰세요.

O____개 X____개

영어	한국어
ago	
ahead	
almost	
already	
big	
cake	
fly	
guitar	
invent	
kite	
left	
listen	
make	
math	
music	
radio	
right	
room	
salt	
small	

한국어	영어
부 이미	
동 만들다	
명 연	
부 앞으로, 앞에	
형 작은	
동 듣다	
명 음악	
형 왼쪽의 부 왼쪽에, 왼쪽으로	
부 거의	
명 기타	
명 케이크	
부 ~전에	
동 날다, 날리다	
명 소금	
형 큰	
동 발명하다	
명 수학	
명 라디오	
명 방	
형 오른쪽의 부 오른쪽으로, 우측으로	

Workbook

Day 05

| 월 일 | 영어 단어에 해당하는 한국어 뜻을 함께 적으세요.

before	~전에	before	~전에
boring	지루한		
safe	안전한		
area	지역		
food	음식		
body	몸, 신체		
leg	다리		
sun	태양		
away	떨어져, 다른 데로		
baby	아기		
dish	요리, 접시		
band	밴드, 악대		
movie	영화		
foot	발		
dangerous	위험한		
autumn	가을		
sunglasses	선글라스		
delicious	맛있는		
bamboo	대나무		
after	~후에		

다음 단어에 해당하는 영어 단어 또는 우리말을 쓰세요.

O____개 X____개

영어	한국어
after	
area	
autumn	
away	
baby	
bamboo	
band	
before	
body	
boring	
dangerous	
delicious	
dish	
food	
foot	
leg	
movie	
safe	
sun	
sunglasses	

한국어	영어
형 위험한	
명 선글라스	
명 아기	
명 가을	
명 다리	
명 음식	
형 지루한	
명 대나무	
전 ~후에	
형 맛있는	
전 ~전에	
명 밴드, 악대	
형 안전한	
명 발	
명 지역	
명 태양	
명 몸, 신체	
명 영화	
명 요리, 접시	
부 떨어져, 다른 데로	

Workbook

Day 06

| 월 일 |

영어 단어에 해당하는 한국어 뜻을 함께 적으세요.

save	절약하다	save	절약하다
money	돈		
brush	빗; 닦다, 빗다		
necklace	목걸이		
bark	짖다; (개, 동물) 짖는 소리		
coat	코트		
jacket	자켓		
seafood	해산물		
pretty	예쁜; 꽤, 매우		
get	타다, 얻다		
lose	잃다, 지다		
smart	똑똑한		
doctor	의사		
choose	선택하다		
dentist	치과 의사		
bar	바, 막대		
barber	이발사		
ring	반지		
basket	바구니		
bath	목욕		

다음 단어에 해당하는 영어 단어 또는 우리말을 쓰세요. O____개 X____개

영어	한국어
bar	
barber	
bark	
basket	
bath	
brush	
choose	
coat	
dentist	
doctor	
get	
jacket	
lose	
money	
necklace	
pretty	
ring	
save	
seafood	
smart	

한국어	영어
명 이발사	
형 똑똑한	
명 치과 의사	
명 바, 막대	
명 자켓	
동 절약하다	
명 바구니	
동 짖다 명 (개, 동물) 짖는 소리	
동 잃다, 지다	
명 의사	
명 반지	
명 해산물	
동 타다, 얻다	
명 코트	
명 목걸이	
명 돈	
명 빗 동 닦다, 빗다	
형 예쁜 부 꽤, 매우	
명 목욕	
동 선택하다	

Workbook

Day 07

| 월 일 |

영어 단어에 해당하는 한국어 뜻을 함께 적으세요.

day	낮, 하루, 날	day	낮, 하루, 날
become	~이 되다		
minute	분		
month	달		
king	왕		
pull	끌다, 잡아 당기다		
soldier	군인, 병사		
princess	공주		
push	누르다, 밀다		
bean	콩		
different	다른		
subject	과목		
science	과학		
flower	꽃		
prince	왕자		
same	같은		
crown	왕관		
beat	치다; 박자		
because	~때문에		
hour	시간		

다음 단어에 해당하는 영어 단어 또는 우리말을 쓰세요. ○____개 ×____개

영어	한국어
bean	
beat	
because	
become	
crown	
day	
different	
flower	
hour	
king	
minute	
month	
prince	
princess	
pull	
push	
same	
science	
soldier	
subject	

한국어	영어
동 치다 명 박자	
명 왕	
명 과목	
동 ~이 되다	
부 같은	
접 ~때문에	
명 군인, 병사	
명 왕관	
명 시간	
명 달	
형 다른	
명 꽃	
동 누르다, 밀다	
명 콩	
명 왕자	
명 과학	
명 낮, 하루, 날	
명 분	
동 끌다, 잡아 당기다	
명 공주	

Workbook

Day 08

| 월 일 |

영어 단어에 해당하는 한국어 뜻을 함께 적으세요.

fix	고치다	fix	고치다
useful	유용한		
box	상자		
hobby	취미		
fresh	신선한		
air	공기		
open	열다; 열린		
cloudy	흐린		
purple	보라색; 보라색의		
vegetable	야채		
use	사용하다		
favorite	가장 좋아하는		
help	도움; 돕다		
bed	침대		
bell	종		
between	~사이에		
board	판, 게시판		
boat	배		
bone	뼈		
ride	타다		

다음 단어에 해당하는 영어 단어 또는 우리말을 쓰세요. O___개 X___개

영어	한국어
air	
bed	
bell	
between	
board	
boat	
bone	
box	
cloudy	
favorite	
fix	
fresh	
help	
hobby	
open	
purple	
ride	
use	
useful	
vegetable	

한국어	영어
동 고치다	
명 야채	
명 취미	
형 가장 좋아하는	
형 신선한	
형 유용한	
명 종	
명 판, 게시판	
전 ~사이에	
동 사용하다	
명 상자	
명 공기	
동 열다 형 열린	
형 흐린	
명 도움 동 돕다	
명 배	
동 타다	
명 뼈	
명 보라색 형 보라색의	
명 침대	

Workbook

Day 09

| 월 일 |

영어 단어에 해당하는 한국어 뜻을 함께 적으세요.

art	미술, 예술	art	미술, 예술
write	쓰다		
buy	사다		
brain	두뇌, 머리		
sing	노래하다		
play	놀다, 게임을 하다, 연주하다		
break	휴식; 깨다		
plant	식물; 심다		
bridge	다리		
sorry	미안한		
future	미래		
wash	씻다		
queen	여왕, 여신		
card	카드		
ticket	표		
brand	브랜드, 상표		
game	게임		
breathe	숨쉬다		
thank	감사; 감사하다		
artist	예술가		

다음 단어에 해당하는 영어 단어 또는 우리말을 쓰세요. O____개 X____개

영어	한국어
art	
artist	
brain	
brand	
break	
breathe	
bridge	
buy	
card	
future	
game	
plant	
play	
queen	
sing	
sorry	
thank	
ticket	
wash	
write	

한국어	영어
명 휴식 동 깨다	
동 감사하다 명 감사	
동 숨쉬다	
형 미안한	
동 쓰다	
명 다리	
명 브랜드, 상표	
명 게임	
동 놀다, 게임을 하다, 연주하다	
명 표	
동 노래하다	
명 식물 동 심다	
명 예술가	
명 미술, 예술	
명 미래	
동 씻다	
명 여왕, 여신	
동 사다	
명 두뇌, 머리	
명 카드	

Workbook

Day 10

| 월 일 |

영어 단어에 해당하는 한국어 뜻을 함께 적으세요.

watch	보다	watch	보다
visit	방문하다		
grandparents	조부모		
hungry	배고픈		
full	가득한, 배가 부른		
thick	두꺼운		
thin	얇은		
family	가족		
cousin	사촌		
mix	섞다		
season	계절		
fall	떨어지다; 가을		
sport	운동		
football	미식 축구		
carry	옮기다, 휴대하다		
nurse	간호사		
camera	카메라		
dead	죽은		
business	사업		
butter	버터		

다음 단어에 해당하는 영어 단어 또는 우리말을 쓰세요.

O ____개 X ____개

영어	한국어
business	
butter	
camera	
carry	
cousin	
dead	
fall	
family	
football	
full	
grandparents	
hungry	
mix	
nurse	
season	
sport	
thick	
thin	
visit	
watch	

한국어	영어
동 옮기다, 휴대하다	
명 조부모	
명 가족	
명 운동	
명 카메라	
명 사업	
명 버터	
명 섞다	
동 방문하다	
명 사촌	
형 얇은	
명 계절	
동 떨어지다 명 가을	
동 보다	
형 배고픈	
형 가득한, 배가 부른	
명 미식 축구	
형 죽은	
명 간호사	
형 두꺼운	

Workbook

Day 11

| 월 일 |

영어 단어에 해당하는 한국어 뜻을 함께 적으세요.

plane	비행기	plane	비행기
slow	느린		
strong	강한		
weak	약한		
go	가다		
pilot	조종사		
chance	기회		
bake	굽다		
congratulate	축하하다		
fast	빠른; 빠르게, 빨리		
warm	따뜻한		
stretch	뻗다		
bye	안녕		
care	돌보다; 돌봄, 보살핌		
center	중심, 중앙		
bring	가져오다		
church	교회		
check	확인하다		
stop	멈추다		
cartoon	만화		

다음 단어에 해당하는 영어 단어 또는 우리말을 쓰세요.

O____개 X____개

영어	한국어
bake	
bring	
bye	
care	
center	
chance	
cartoon	
check	
church	
congratulate	
fast	
go	
pilot	
plane	
slow	
stop	
stretch	
strong	
warm	
weak	

한국어	영어
동 멈추다	
명 비행기	
동 가다	
형 따뜻한	
명 교회	
동 뻗다	
동 가져오다	
형 약한	
감 안녕	
명 기회	
동 굽다	
명 조종사	
형 강한	
동 돌보다 명 돌봄, 보살핌	
명 만화	
동 축하하다	
형 빠른 부 빠르게, 빨리	
동 확인하다	
명 중심, 중앙	
형 느린	

Workbook

Day 12

| 월 일 | 영어 단어에 해당하는 한국어 뜻을 함께 적으세요.

date	날짜, 데이트	date	날짜, 데이트
drive	운전하다		
brave	용감한		
brown	갈색의; 갈색		
aunt	이모, 숙모, 고모		
butterfly	나비		
chew	씹다		
introduce	소개하다		
jump	뛰다		
off	떨어져, (무엇이) 제거되어		
homework	숙제		
surf	파도타기를 하다, 인터넷을 검색하다		
enjoy	즐기다		
party	파티		
corner	모퉁이		
curly	구불구불한		
curtain	커튼		
bright	밝은, 똑똑한		
deep	깊은		
scary	무서운		

다음 단어에 해당하는 영어 단어 또는 우리말을 쓰세요. ○____개 ✕____개

영어	한국어
aunt	
brave	
bright	
brown	
butterfly	
chew	
corner	
curly	
curtain	
date	
deep	
drive	
enjoy	
off	
homework	
introduce	
jump	
party	
scary	
surf	

한국어	영어
명 이모, 숙모, 고모	
명 커튼	
명 숙제	
동 소개하다	
형 무서운	
형 구불구불한	
부 떨어져, (무엇이) 제거되어	
형 용감한	
명 파티	
동 운전하다	
동 즐기다	
명 날짜, 데이트	
동 뛰다	
동 파도타기를 하다, 인터넷을 검색하다	
형 깊은	
형 밝은, 똑똑한	
형 갈색의 명 갈색	
명 나비	
명 모퉁이	
동 씹다	

Workbook

Day 13

| 월 일 |

영어 단어에 해당하는 한국어 뜻을 함께 적으세요.

country	나라, 시골	country	나라, 시골
doll	인형		
busy	바쁜		
free	자유로운		
early	이른; 일찍		
late	늦은; 늦게		
round	둥근		
live	살다		
back	뒤; 다시 돌아와서		
ball	공		
circle	원		
ready	준비가 된		
newspaper	신문		
read	읽다		
whole	전체의		
noon	낮 12시, 정오		
wish	소원; 바라다, 원하다		
world	세계		
worry	걱정하다; 걱정, 근심		
together	함께, 같이		

다음 단어에 해당하는 영어 단어 또는 우리말을 쓰세요.

○____개 ×____개

영어	한국어
back	
ball	
busy	
circle	
country	
doll	
early	
free	
late	
live	
newspaper	
noon	
read	
ready	
round	
together	
whole	
wish	
world	
worry	

한국어	영어
명 나라, 시골	
형 자유로운	
명 인형	
형 준비가 된	
명 소원 동 바라다, 원하다	
부 함께, 같이	
형 바쁜	
동 걱정하다 명 걱정, 근심	
형 이른 부 일찍	
명 뒤 부 다시 돌아와서	
동 읽다	
형 늦은 부 늦게	
명 신문	
형 전체의	
형 둥근	
명 원	
명 살다	
명 세계	
명 낮 12시, 정오	
명 공	

Workbook

Day 14

| 월 일 |

영어 단어에 해당하는 한국어 뜻을 함께 적으세요.

poor	가난한, 불쌍한	poor	가난한, 불쌍한
sweet	달콤한		
laugh	웃음; 웃다		
duck	오리		
candy	사탕		
spicy	매운		
look	보다		
fan	팬, 선풍기		
upset	속상한		
win	이기다		
pay	지불하다		
child	아이		
tooth	이, 치아		
drop	방울; 떨어뜨리다		
factory	공장		
rich	부유한		
excuse	변명; 변명하다, 용서하다		
errand	심부름		
famous	유명한		
behind	뒤에; 뒤로, 뒤에		

다음 단어에 해당하는 영어 단어 또는 우리말을 쓰세요.

○____개 ✕____개

영어	한국어
behind	
candy	
child	
drop	
duck	
errand	
excuse	
factory	
famous	
fan	
laugh	
look	
pay	
poor	
rich	
spicy	
sweet	
tooth	
upset	
win	

한국어	영어
명 방울 동 떨어뜨리다	
명 공장	
동 보다	
명 이기다	
명 이, 치아	
형 매운	
명 변명 동 변명하다, 용서하다	
형 가난한,불쌍한	
형 속상한	
형 달콤한	
명 사탕	
명 뒤에 부 뒤로, 뒤에	
형 유명한	
형 부유한	
명 팬, 선풍기	
명 웃음 동 웃다	
명 아이	
동 지불하다	
명 심부름	
명 오리	

Workbook

Day 15 | 월 일 |

영어 단어에 해당하는 한국어 뜻을 함께 적으세요.

red	붉은; 빨강, 빨간색	red	붉은; 빨강, 빨간색
blood	피		
block	큰 덩어리, 한 구획		
thing	물건		
monkey	원숭이		
train	기차		
contest	경연, 대회		
keep	유지하다, 보유하다		
secret	비밀; 비밀의		
bad	나쁜		
near	~근처에; 가까이		
earth	지구		
tradition	전통		
yet	아직		
textbook	교과서		
theater	극장		
then	그때		
piece	조각		
throat	목구멍		
tomorrow	내일		

다음 단어에 해당하는 영어 단어 또는 우리말을 쓰세요.

O____개 X____개

영어	한국어
bad	
block	
blood	
contest	
earth	
keep	
monkey	
near	
piece	
red	
secret	
textbook	
theater	
then	
thing	
throat	
tomorrow	
tradition	
train	
yet	

한국어	영어
명 극장	
형 붉은 명 빨강, 빨간색	
명 경연, 대회	
명 비밀 형 비밀의	
명 원숭이	
명 물건	
명 내일	
명 전통	
명 교과서	
명 피	
명 큰 덩어리, 한 구획	
부 아직	
형 나쁜	
명 목구멍	
전 ~근처에 부 가까이	
동 유지하다, 보유하다	
명 조각	
부 그때	
명 지구	
명 기차	

Workbook

Day 16

| 월 일 |

영어 단어에 해당하는 한국어 뜻을 함께 적으세요.

work	일하다; 일, 작업	work	일하다; 일, 작업
rest	휴식; 쉬다		
park	공원		
swim	수영; 수영하다		
beach	해변		
oven	오븐		
restaurant	식당		
president	대통령, 회장		
student	학생		
design	디자인; 디자인하다		
moon	달		
office	사무실		
often	종종, 자주		
pool	물 웅덩이		
only	유일한; 단지		
orange	오렌지		
meal	식사		
seat	자리, 좌석		
parade	행진, 퍼레이드		
awake	깨어있는; 깨다		

다음 단어에 해당하는 영어 단어 또는 우리말을 쓰세요.

O____개 X____개

영어	한국어
awake	
beach	
design	
meal	
moon	
office	
often	
only	
orange	
oven	
parade	
park	
pool	
president	
rest	
restaurant	
seat	
student	
swim	
work	

한국어	영어
부 종종, 자주	
동 일하다 명 일, 작업	
명 사무실	
명 물 웅덩이	
명 식당	
명 오렌지	
명 해변	
명 식사	
형 유일한 부 단지	
형 깨어있는 동 깨다	
명 공원	
명 휴식 동 쉬다	
명 달	
명 자리, 좌석	
명 수영 동 수영하다	
명 대통령, 회장	
명 학생	
명 오븐	
명 디자인 동 디자인하다	
명 행진, 퍼레이드	

Workbook

Day 17

| 월 일 |

영어 단어에 해당하는 한국어 뜻을 함께 적으세요.

top	꼭대기, 정상	top	꼭대기, 정상
see	보다		
blind	시각 장애의		
police	경찰		
fire	불		
paint	색을 칠하다		
wall	벽		
rock	바위		
stick	막대기		
treat	대접; 대하다, 대접하다		
airport	공항		
museum	박물관		
sick	아픈		
everything	모든 것		
tonight	오늘 밤; 오늘 밤에		
touch	만지다, 접촉하다; 연락, 접촉		
towel	수건		
tower	탑		
ship	배		
shoulder	어깨		

다음 단어에 해당하는 영어 단어 또는 우리말을 쓰세요.

O____개 X____개

영어	한국어
airport	
blind	
everything	
fire	
museum	
paint	
police	
rock	
see	
ship	
shoulder	
sick	
stick	
tonight	
top	
touch	
towel	
tower	
treat	
wall	

한국어	영어
명 어깨	
명 바위	
명 경찰	
명 막대기	
명 보다	
명 공항	
명 수건	
명 배	
명 벽	
명 오늘 밤	
명 대접 동 대하다, 대접하다	
명 불	
명 꼭대기, 정상	
명 탑	
동 색을 칠하다	
명 박물관	
형 시각 장애의	
대 모든 것	
형 아픈	
동 만지다, 접촉하다 명 연락, 접촉	

Workbook

Day 18

| 월 일 |

영어 단어에 해당하는 한국어 뜻을 함께 적으세요.

heavy	무거운	heavy	무거운
closet	옷장		
snack	간식		
window	창문		
ask	묻다, 부탁하다		
price	가격, 값		
problem	문제		
drink	마시다; 음료		
once	한 번, 한때		
peach	복숭아		
second	두 번째의		
grow	성장하다, 자라다		
goat	염소		
house	집		
twice	두 번		
pea	완두콩		
peace	평화, 평온함		
first	처음, 최초, 첫째; 처음의		
smile	웃음; 웃다		
wide	넓은		

다음 단어에 해당하는 영어 단어 또는 우리말을 쓰세요.

O____개 X____개

영어	한국어
ask	
closet	
drink	
first	
goat	
grow	
heavy	
house	
once	
pea	
peace	
peach	
price	
problem	
second	
smile	
snack	
twice	
wide	
window	

한국어	영어
명 가격, 값	
부 두 번	
명 염소	
형 두 번째의	
명 완두콩	
명 평화, 평온함	
동 마시다 명 음료	
명 옷장	
명 웃음 동 웃다	
명 창문	
명 간식	
명 복숭아	
동 성장하다, 자라다	
명 처음, 최초, 첫째 형 처음의	
동 묻다, 부탁하다	
명 집	
부 한 번, 한때	
명 문제	
형 무거운	
형 넓은	

Workbook

Day 19

| 월 일 |

영어 단어에 해당하는 한국어 뜻을 함께 적으세요.

wear	입다	wear	입다
shirt	셔츠		
catch	붙잡다		
pocket	주머니		
city	도시		
power	힘		
sit	앉다		
week	주		
usually	보통, 대개		
map	지도		
exercise	운동; 운동하다		
gym	체육관		
pumpkin	호박		
library	도서관		
word	단어		
dictionary	사전		
sometimes	때때로		
soap	비누		
guide	안내자, 안내(서)		
feel	느끼다; 느낌		

다음 단어에 해당하는 영어 단어 또는 우리말을 쓰세요.

○____개 ×____개

영어	한국어
catch	
city	
dictionary	
exercise	
feel	
guide	
gym	
library	
map	
pocket	
power	
pumpkin	
shirt	
sit	
soap	
sometimes	
usually	
wear	
week	
word	

한국어	영어
명 사전	
명 단어	
동 느끼다 명 느낌	
부 때때로	
명 셔츠	
부 보통, 대개	
명 도시	
명 주	
동 앉다	
명 힘	
명 도서관	
명 운동 동 운동하다	
명 비누	
동 붙잡다	
명 호박	
명 체육관	
동 입다	
명 주머니	
명 안내자, 안내(서)	
명 지도	

Day 20

| 월 일 |

영어 단어에 해당하는 한국어 뜻을 함께 적으세요.

horse	말	horse	말
race	경주		
shoe	신발		
feed	먹이를 주다, 먹이다, 먹여 키우다		
holiday	휴일		
town	마을, 소도시		
afternoon	오후		
fever	열, 열병		
cough	기침; 기침하다		
windy	바람이 부는		
young	어린, 젊은		
old	오래된, 나이 든		
straight	곧은		
bend	구부리다		
store	상점		
moment	순간		
notebook	공책,수첩		
energy	에너지, 힘		
festival	축제		
fight	싸우다; 싸움		

다음 단어에 해당하는 영어 단어 또는 우리말을 쓰세요.

O____개 X____개

영어	한국어
afternoon	
bend	
cough	
energy	
feed	
festival	
fever	
fight	
holiday	
horse	
moment	
notebook	
old	
race	
shoe	
store	
straight	
town	
windy	
young	

한국어	영어
명 휴일	
명 오후	
명 경주	
명 에너지, 힘	
명 말	
동 구부리다	
명 기침 동 기침하다	
형 오래된, 나이 든	
명 공책,수첩	
동 먹이를 주다, 먹이다, 먹여 키우다	
명 마을	
명 상점	
형 바람이 부는	
형 어린, 젊은	
명 순간	
형 곧은	
명 신발	
명 축제	
동 싸우다 명 싸움	
명 열, 열병	

Workbook

Day 21

| 월 일 |

영어 단어에 해당하는 한국어 뜻을 함께 적으세요.

farm	농장	farm	농장
hospital	병원		
follow	따르다		
add	더하다		
need	필요하다		
medicine	약		
mirror	거울		
goal	목표, 득점		
throw	던지다		
forest	숲		
bread	빵		
pillow	베개		
station	역, 기관		
pear	배		
pencil	연필		
find	찾다		
flag	깃발		
flu	독감		
invite	초대하다		
turn	돌리다, 돌다		

다음 단어에 해당하는 영어 단어 또는 우리말을 쓰세요.　　　　○____개 ✕____개

영어	한국어
add	
bread	
farm	
find	
flag	
flu	
follow	
forest	
goal	
hospital	
invite	
medicine	
mirror	
need	
pear	
pencil	
pillow	
station	
throw	
turn	

한국어	영어
명 연필	
동 더하다	
명 깃발	
동 따르다	
명 약	
명 거울	
명 배	
동 초대하다	
명 목표, 득점	
명 독감	
명 빵	
동 찾다	
명 농장	
동 던지다	
명 역, 기관	
동 돌리다, 돌다	
명 병원	
명 숲	
명 베개	
동 필요하다	

Workbook

Day 22

| 월 일 | 영어 단어에 해당하는 한국어 뜻을 함께 적으세요.

take	타다, 사진을 찍다	take	타다, 사진을 찍다
picture	그림, 사진		
pass	지나가다, 건네주다, (시험을) 통과하다		
practice	연습; 연습하다		
travel	여행; 여행가다		
bee	벌		
honey	꿀		
lovely	사랑스러운, 멋진		
bank	은행		
pig	돼지		
post office	우체국		
runny	콧물이 나는, 묽은		
quiz	퀴즈		
history	역사		
fork	포크		
from	~로 부터		
fun	재미있는; 재미, 즐거움		
speak	말하다		
gift	선물		
give	주다		

다음 단어에 해당하는 영어 단어 또는 우리말을 쓰세요. ○____개 ✕____개

영어	한국어
bank	
bee	
fork	
from	
fun	
gift	
give	
history	
honey	
lovely	
pass	
picture	
pig	
post office	
practice	
quiz	
runny	
speak	
take	
travel	

한국어	영어
명 벌	
동 말하다	
명 꿀	
명 연습 동 연습하다	
명 선물	
명 역사	
명 포크	
전 ~로 부터	
형 사랑스러운,멋진	
형 콧물이 나는, 묽은	
명 퀴즈	
명 여행 동 여행가다	
명 그림, 사진	
명 은행	
명 우체국	
형 재미있는 명 재미, 즐거움	
명 돼지	
동 지나가다, 건네주다, (시험을) 통과하다	
동 주다	
동 타다, 사진을 찍다	

Workbook

Day 23

| 월 일 |

영어 단어에 해당하는 한국어 뜻을 함께 적으세요.

pair	쌍, 켤레	pair	쌍, 켤레
bottle	병		
stove	난로		
magic	마법		
tall	키가 큰		
pink	분홍의; 분홍색		
building	건물		
daughter	딸		
son	아들		
brother	남자 형제		
have	가지고 있다		
glue	풀		
grade	학년, 성적		
grammar	문법		
habit	습관		
hall	강당, 홀		
hamburger	햄버거		
happen	발생하다, 일어나다		
hat	모자		
sister	여자 형제		

다음 단어에 해당하는 영어 단어 또는 우리말을 쓰세요. O____개 X____개

영어	한국어	한국어	영어
bottle		명 마법	
brother		명 강당, 홀	
building		명 습관	
daughter		형 분홍의 명 분홍색	
glue		형 쌍, 켤레	
grade		명 난로	
grammar		명 햄버거	
habit		명 병	
hall		명 모자	
hamburger		명 아들	
happen		명 학년, 성적	
hat		명 딸	
have		동 발생하다, 일어나다	
magic		명 문법	
pair		명 남자 형제	
pink		동 가지고 있다	
sister		명 여자 형제	
son		형 키가 큰	
stove		명 건물	
tall		명 풀	

Workbook

Day 24

| 월 일 | 영어 단어에 해당하는 한국어 뜻을 함께 적으세요.

interesting	재미있는, 흥미로운	interesting	재미있는, 흥미로운
like	좋아하다		
over	넘어서, ~위에		
vacation	휴가, 방학		
baseball	야구		
basketball	농구		
year	해, 년		
trip	여행		
wise	지혜로운		
pet	애완동물		
pick	고르다, 줍다, 따다		
program	프로그램, 계획		
put	놓다, 향하게 하다		
subway	지하철		
sure	확신하는		
surprise	놀라운 일; 놀라게 하다		
sound	소리; ~처럼 들리다		
health	건강		
hen	암탉		
here	여기에		

다음 단어에 해당하는 영어 단어 또는 우리말을 쓰세요.

O____개 X____개

영어	한국어
baseball	
basketball	
health	
hen	
here	
interesting	
like	
over	
pet	
pick	
program	
put	
sound	
subway	
sure	
surprise	
trip	
vacation	
wise	
year	

한국어	영어
동 고르다, 줍다, 따다	
명 휴가, 방학	
명 야구	
형 확신하는	
명 놀라운 일 동 놀라게 하다	
명 건강	
명 애완동물	
명 프로그램, 계획	
동 좋아하다	
명 지하철	
형 지혜로운	
명 여기에	
명 해, 년	
형 재미있는, 흥미로운	
명 여행	
명 암탉	
동 놓다, 향하게 하다	
전 넘어서, ~위에	
명 농구	
명 소리 동 ~처럼 들리다	

Workbook
Day 25

| 월 일 |

영어 단어에 해당하는 한국어 뜻을 함께 적으세요.

kind	친절한; 종류	kind	친절한; 종류
great	좋은, 훌륭한		
little	작은, 어린		
lesson	수업, 교훈		
plastic	플라스틱으로 된; 플라스틱		
shop	가게		
society	사회		
hope	희망하다; 희망		
cut	자르다		
onion	양파		
mail	편지, 우편		
send	보내다		
hike	도보 여행을 하다		
hit	때리다, 치다		
hold	잡고 있다, 열다		
hometown	고향		
hundred	백		
hurt	다치다; 아픈		
husband	남편		
idea	생각		

다음 단어에 해당하는 영어 단어 또는 우리말을 쓰세요.

○___개 ×___개

영어	한국어
cut	
great	
hike	
hit	
hold	
hometown	
hope	
hundred	
hurt	
husband	
idea	
kind	
lesson	
little	
mail	
onion	
plastic	
send	
shop	
society	

한국어	영어
형 플라스틱으로 된 명 플라스틱	
명 수업, 교훈	
동 희망하다 명 희망	
명 고향	
명 남편	
형 좋은, 훌륭한	
형 작은, 어린	
동 때리다, 치다	
형 친절한 명 종류	
명 사회	
동 보내다	
명 가게	
명 생각	
동 다치다	
명 백	
동 자르다	
동 잡고 있다, 열다	
동 도보 여행을 하다	
명 편지, 우편	
명 양파	

Workbook

Day 26 | 월 일 |

영어 단어에 해당하는 한국어 뜻을 함께 적으세요.

life	삶, 인생	life	삶, 인생
sheep	양		
mistake	실수		
street	거리		
camel	낙타		
lake	호수		
blow	불다		
balloon	풍선		
answer	답, 대답; 답하다		
kid	아이		
come	오다		
print	인쇄하다; 인쇄물, 인쇄		
island	섬		
joke	놀리다; 농담		
just	막, 단지		
question	질문		
knee	무릎		
knit	뜨다, 짜다		
know	알다		
lady	숙녀		

다음 단어에 해당하는 영어 단어 또는 우리말을 쓰세요.

O____개 X____개

영어	한국어
answer	
balloon	
blow	
camel	
come	
island	
joke	
just	
kid	
knee	
knit	
know	
lady	
lake	
life	
mistake	
print	
question	
sheep	
street	

한국어	영어
명 실수	
명 무릎	
명 거리	
명 양	
명 섬	
동 놀리다 명 농담	
동 불다	
명 호수	
명 답, 대답 동 답하다	
동 알다	
명 풍선	
명 숙녀	
동 오다	
동 인쇄하다 명 인쇄물	
부 막, 단지	
명 질문	
명 아이	
동 뜨다, 짜다	
명 낙타	
명 삶, 인생	

Workbook

Day 27

| 월 일 |

영어 단어에 해당하는 한국어 뜻을 함께 적으세요.

count	세다	count	세다
number	숫자		
taste	맛; 맛보다, 맛이 나다		
miss	놓치다		
member	회원		
glad	기쁜		
weigh	무게를 재다, 무게가 나가다		
serve	제공하다		
yesterday	어제		
high	높은; 높이		
people	사람들		
oil	기름		
later	후에, 나중에		
spell	철자를 쓰다		
learn	배우다		
leave	떠나다, 출발하다		
magazine	잡지		
main	주요한, 주된		
many	많은		
market	시장		

다음 단어에 해당하는 영어 단어 또는 우리말을 쓰세요.

○____개 ×____개

영어	한국어
count	
glad	
later	
learn	
leave	
magazine	
main	
many	
market	
member	
miss	
number	
off	
oil	
people	
serve	
spell	
taste	
weigh	
yesterday	

한국어	영어
명 회원	
동 놓치다	
명 시장	
형 주요한, 주된	
동 제공하다	
동 철자를 쓰다	
동 떠나다, 출발하다	
명 기름	
동 무게를 재다, 무게가 나가다	
동 배우다	
부 어제	
부 후에, 나중에	
명 맛 동 맛보다, 맛이 나다	
형 많은	
명 세다	
형 기쁜	
명 잡지	
명 사람들	
형 높은 부 높이	
명 숫자	

Workbook

Day 28

| 월 일 |

영어 단어에 해당하는 한국어 뜻을 함께 적으세요.

think	생각하다	think	생각하다
cover	덮다, 가리다; 덮개, 표지		
each	각각의; 각각		
all	모든; 모두		
start	시작하다		
finish	마치다		
angel	천사		
hurry	서두르다; 서두름, 급함		
say	말하다		
simple	간단한		
weekend	주말		
welcome	환영하는; 환영하다		
every	모든		
letter	편지		
hill	언덕, (나지막한) 산, 경사로		
marry	~와 결혼하다		
mask	가면		
match	경기		
matter	문제		
may	~해도 좋다		

다음 단어에 해당하는 영어 단어 또는 우리말을 쓰세요.

O____개 X____개

영어	한국어
all	
angel	
cover	
each	
every	
finish	
hill	
hurry	
letter	
marry	
mask	
match	
matter	
may	
say	
simple	
start	
think	
weekend	
welcome	

한국어	영어
형 환영하는 동 환영하다	
조 ~해도 좋다	
동 생각하다	
동 덮다, 가리다 명 덮개, 표지	
명 가면	
동 서두르다 명 서두름, 급함	
동 마치다	
형 각각의 대 각각	
명 언덕, (나지막한) 산, 경사로	
동 시작하다	
형 모든 대 모두	
명 문제	
명 편지	
형 간단한	
동 ~와 결혼하다	
명 주말	
명 천사	
명 경기	
동 말하다	
형 모든	

Day 29

| 월 일 |

영어 단어에 해당하는 한국어 뜻을 함께 적으세요.

bite	물다; 물기, 무는 것	bite	물다; 물기, 무는 것
mountain	산		
comic	웃기는, 재미있는, 만화의		
large	큰, 거대한		
size	크기		
smell	냄새를 맡다; 냄새		
hear	듣다		
try	노력하다, ~해보다		
name	이름		
elephant	코끼리		
fox	여우		
neck	목, 목 부분		
milk	우유		
nest	둥지		
new	새로운		
nice	좋은, 멋진		
now	지금, 이제		
meat	고기		
meet	만나다		
luck	운, 운수		

다음 단어에 해당하는 영어 단어 또는 우리말을 쓰세요.

O____개 X____개

영어	한국어
bite	
comic	
elephant	
fox	
hear	
large	
luck	
meat	
meet	
milk	
mountain	
name	
neck	
nest	
new	
nice	
now	
size	
smell	
try	

한국어	영어
형 새로운	
명 운, 운수	
명 여우	
동 냄새를 맡다 명 냄새	
명 코끼리	
명 산	
동 듣다	
동 물다 명 물기, 무는 것	
형 웃기는, 재미있는, 만화의	
명 둥지	
부 지금, 이제	
명 이름	
명 목, 목 부분	
동 만나다	
형 좋은, 멋진	
명 크기	
명 우유	
동 노력하다, ~해보다	
명 고기	
형 큰, 거대한	

Workbook

Day 30

| 월 일 |

영어 단어에 해당하는 한국어 뜻을 함께 적으세요.

iron	철, 다리미	iron	철, 다리미
share	공유하다		
terrible	심각한		
real	실제의		
perfect	완벽한		
repeat	반복하다		
sink	싱크대; 가라앉다		
ant	개미		
potato	감자		
turtle	거북이		
professor	교수		
abroad	외국에		
present	선물, 현재		
kick	차다		
sell	팔다		
toilet	화장실		
sea	바다		
study	공부; 공부하다		
garden	정원		
place	장소		

다음 단어에 해당하는 영어 단어 또는 우리말을 쓰세요. ○____개 ×____개

영어	한국어
abroad	
ant	
garden	
kick	
perfect	
place	
potato	
present	
professor	
real	
repeat	
iron	
sea	
sell	
share	
sink	
study	
terrible	
toilet	
turtle	

한국어	영어
동 공유하다	
형 심각한	
명 철, 다리미	
동 반복하다	
명 화장실	
형 실제의	
명 싱크대 동 가라앉다	
형 완벽한	
명 개미	
부 외국에	
명 바다	
명 거북이	
명 장소	
명 교수	
명 차다	
명 감자	
명 선물, 현재	
명 정원	
동 팔다	
명 공부 동 공부하다	

memo

memo

30일 완성 내신 • 수능 완전 정복! **Word Max** 6단계 시리즈

WORD MAX
5300

MP3 무료 다운로드 www.wcbooks.co.kr

WorldCom Edu